Scotland's leading educational publishers

D0243297

CfE Higher
BUSINESS MANAGEMENT
COURSE NOTES

Lee Coutts

Chapter 1

UNIT 1 – Understanding Business

Chapter 2

Chapter 3

End of unit material

UNIT 2 – Management of People and Finance

Chapter 4

Chapter 5

End of unit material

UNIT 3 – Management of Marketing and Operations

Chapter 6

Chapter 7

End of unit material

Case study answers

1 Get Set for Learning

What you will learn in this chapter:

- The structure of these Course Notes.
- The structure of the Higher Business Management course.
- The differences between Higher and National 5 Business Management.
- The skills you will develop when studying Higher Business Management.

Welcome to your Course Notes!

These Course Notes are designed specifically for those undertaking Higher Business Management. They are designed to help you learn as much as you can in Higher Business Management and to do as well as you can in your assessments and exams. They encourage you to think about your learning and to develop Skills for Life, Work and Learning.

There are 2 chapters per Unit in these Course Notes and each chapter focuses on a specific learning outcome. A learning outcome is what you should be able to do once you have completed it – you will be assessed on this.

Unit 1 – Understanding Business

Learning Outcome	Chapter
1. Analyse the features, objectives and internal structures of large business organisations.	• 2-Business Organisations
2. Analyse the environment in which large organisations operate.	• 3-Business Environment

Unit 2 – Management of People and Finance

1. Apply knowledge and understanding of how the management of people can meet the objectives of large organisations.	• 4-Management of People
2. Apply knowledge and understanding of how the management of finance contributes to the effectiveness of large organisations.	• 5-Management of Finance

Unit 3 – Management of Marketing and Operations

1. Apply knowledge and understanding of how the marketing function enhances the effectiveness of large organisations.	• 6-Management of Marketing
2. Apply knowledge and understanding of how the operations function contributes to the success of large organisations.	• 7-Management of Operations

Throughout these Course Notes you will have the opportunity to apply what you have learned by answering questions on different case studies.

Structure of these Course Notes

The structure of these Course Notes is the same throughout.

At the beginning of each Unit, there is an introductory section explaining what you will learn in that Unit.

Each chapter begins with a list of what you should already know about business and a list of learning intentions: this is what you will learn in this chapter. While it is not essential to have studied National 5 Business Management before Higher, it is helpful. If you haven't studied National 5, it might be a good idea to obtain a copy of the National 5 Business Management Course Notes so that you can gain an understanding of how small to medium sized organisations work. These Course Notes are specifically for Higher and do not cover material taught at National 5.

Throughout each chapter there are a number of activities, quick questions, case studies and key questions for you to answer.

- **Activities** are designed to get you to apply the knowledge you have just learned in different situations. You will do these either individually, in pairs, in groups or as a class. Each activity has a list of skills that the activity will develop. These skills will be very useful to you, not just in this course, but for life, work and future learning. See page 7 for further information.

- **Quick questions** are designed to test your knowledge of what you have learned. Some questions are easier than others but they give you the opportunity to think about what you have learned.

- **Case studies** are all real examples of large businesses. They contain a short amount of text to read, followed by questions. These case studies are excellent preparation for your Course Assessment because they get you thinking carefully about the business under discussion and looking at the case study for answers.

- **Key questions** confirm that you have grasped the main points of the chapter. Being able to answer these should help you feel confident for the Unit Assessment.

At the end of each Unit, you will find information on the **Unit Assessment**, sample **exam-style questions** (with comments from an experienced examiner) and a traffic-light **self-assessment checklist**.

Throughout the book there are **watch points** that provide you with advice to help your learning and **make the link** boxes that try to get you to connect what you are learning to other parts of the course and to other subjects. There are also prompts for when you should go back and review material covered at National 5.

These Course Notes contain lots of opportunities for you to work with other people, to use technology and to be creative. They will allow you to learn as much as you can!

Your learning journal

You will be asked to keep a learning journal throughout your Higher Business Management course. This journal is not part of your formal assessment, but will get you thinking about your learning and is a place where you can keep different things that you have learned. It will help you to develop your research and literacy skills, as well as to improve your knowledge of Business Management. At this level, it is crucial that you are able to carry out your own research, evaluate different sources of information and use business terminology correctly. Your learning journal will help you do this.

Your learning journal could take a number of formats – you can decide how you want it to look. You might simply use a jotter to record things and stick things into or you might have a folder that you could use. You could also keep an online blog or journal that records what you are learning.

In your learning journal you should:

- Reflect on your learning as you complete each activity. Think about what you learned, how you learned it and what you still need to work on. Think about the different skills you had to use and what skills you developed.

- Keep copies of relevant newspaper articles or internet printouts/screen shots that you have read – write down next to each one why it was relevant and what you learned from it. You should also think about the strengths and weaknesses of that source of information. This will help you to interpret different sources and to think about the quality of the information you are reading. (This will be excellent preparation for undertaking your Course Assessment.)

- Write about what you heard on the news that is relevant to what you are learning in Business Management. Make a note about the report you listened to and what you learned from it. Again, comment on the quality of the source and note down anything you would question from what you have heard.

- Record when you have engaged with a real business as part of your course, for example, if your class visited a business or you had a guest speaker talking to your class. Note down what you learned, what you enjoyed and anything you need to research further.

- Make a list of key words/concepts that you have learned in class and what these mean – this will make an excellent revision tool when revising for assessments. You could add to your list after every Business Management class. If you still have your list from National 5, you can add the new Higher key words you have learned.

Your learning journal will be something that you can look at throughout your course, and you could even take it to a job or college interview to show them what you have been learning.

The first task for your learning journal appears on page 9.

Higher Business Management

By now, you will know that Business Management is relevant to everybody, no matter what route their life is taking. We all come into contact with business on a daily basis, from using public transport to buying something in a shop or deciding to invest. Business has a powerful influence (positive and negative) on us, the economy and the world.

This course will enable you to understand how contemporary business organisations operate and the activities that they undertake. It focuses on businesses that are large, with a large business being defined as one with more than 250 employees. It considers the complex environment businesses work within and the decisions that they have to take to be successful. Higher Business Management builds on material that was covered at National 5 and the skills that were developed.

The course consists of three Units and two pieces of Course Assessment. The three Units are:

- Understanding Business
- Management of People and Finance
- Management of Marketing and Operations

Higher is at SCQF level 6 and this course is worth 24 SCQF credit points. SCQF is the name given to the framework used to describe qualifications in Scotland. SCQF level 6 describes the level of difficulty of the course and the points are how long the course will take to complete with 1 point = 10 hours of learning. Every Higher course is at SCQF level 6 and contains 24 credit points.

Assessment

Your Teacher/Lecturer will provide you with feedback regularly to let you know how well you are learning the topics in the course. You will also have the opportunity to get feedback from your peers and to reflect on your own learning. Your learning journal can be used to track your progress throughout the course and you can record your feelings and experiences as you go along.

Because this course is certificated by the Scottish Qualifications Authority, you have to undertake formal assessments that will be used to demonstrate that you have achieved each learning outcome as well as the overall course aims.

Unit Assessment

Each Unit will have a formal assessment that you will have to undertake. This can take a number of different formats including extended response questions, a practical task or project, multiple-choice questions or a case study. Your Teacher/Lecturer will explain each Unit's assessment to you and when it will be undertaken. All Unit Assessments are on a pass/fail basis only.

Course Assessment

The Course Assessment allows you to demonstrate that you have achieved the aims of the course and allows you to demonstrate added value. Added value means that you are able to use your knowledge and skills in different and often complex situations. The Course Assessment provides you with an overall grade (A–D or No Award) for the Higher Business Management course. The grade is based on the overall mark you achieve for the Course Assessment out of 100.

The Course Assessment for Higher Business Management consists of two parts:

Question Paper This is worth 70 marks of the Course Assessment	This is an end-of-course examination. The exam is set and marked by the SQA. It is closed-book and you will not know in advance what topics will be assessed. It assesses breadth and application of what you have learned in the course. You will be required to read a substantial case study as part of the exam. The exam will last 2 hours and 15 minutes.
Assignment This is worth 30 marks of the Course Assessment	The assignment will require you to undertake research on an organisation of your choice and to present your findings as a business report. You will have to show that you can research, analyse, evaluate and make decisions. It is designed to be challenging and to get you really thinking about what you have learned.

Skills for Learning, Life and Work

Throughout the course, and this book, you are given opportunities to develop Skills for Learning, Life and Work. These are general skills that you need for your future. The activities in this book are designed to address a number of skills and these are highlighted to you. These will also help prepare you for the Course Assessment. The skills you will develop are:

Numeracy	This involves you using numbers and creating/interpreting graphical information. This is mainly developed in the Management of Finance chapter of this book.
Employability	This is to do with the work-related skills that employers are looking for, which can be used in a job. It is also about helping you to become more familiar with the different careers and opportunities available to you.
ICT (Information and communications technology)	This involves you using technology for learning. You will be given the opportunity to use lots of technology to help you learn, including modern technologies such as Web 2.0 and mobile technologies.

(continued)

Thinking	This involves you being able to think about an issue and the impact or consequences it might have. It also involves you reflecting on something you have done and thinking about how well it went.
Decision-making	This means making a choice. You might be presented with information and have to make a choice. When making decisions, you should be able to give reasons for your choice.
Enterprise	This skill is about being creative and coming up with new ideas. It involves applying what you have learned in new and innovative contexts.
Communication	This means being able to talk to other people. You might be asked to do this in writing or orally, but both are equally important. You need to be able to put your point of view across and to present facts. You also need to be able to listen to other views. When communicating, you should use appropriate business terms as often as you can.
Research	This skill involves you finding something out. This might involve using a number of sources such as the internet, books or people. You should use good quality sources of information and learn how to evaluate them. Remember, not all sources of information contain correct information and you will learn not just to accept facts without sometimes questioning them. This skill will be very important to you when undertaking your assignment for this course.

GO! Individual activity

You are required to keep a learning journal throughout the Business Management course. Page 4 provides more information about what this should contain. To get started you should:

1. Decide what format your learning journal will take – will it be a jotter, a folder or electronic (eg using a blog or online journal)?

2. Start your learning journal by creating a front cover or setting up your blog/journal ready to write in.

Answer the following questions at the beginning of your learning journal:

1. Why have you chosen the format for your journal that you did?

2. What do you want to get from studying Higher Business Management?

3. How will you try to achieve what you want to get from the course?

4. What extra demand will Higher place on you compared to National 5?

Remember, your learning journal is a record of your learning journey throughout this course. This book contains prompts to remind you to record things, but you should feel free to write as much as you can about your learning in Business Management. Your Teacher/Lecturer will ask to see it on a regular basis to make sure you are keeping it up-to-date and professional.

Skills

- Decision-making
- Thinking
- ICT

Unit 1

Understanding Business

2 Business Organisations

The role of business in society

Sectors of industry

Primary
Businesses in the primary sector extract raw materials from the ground. These businesses include agriculture, fishing, oil and gas extraction, and mining.

Secondary
Businesses in this sector manufacture goods. They take raw materials and transform them into a tangible, finished product. Examples include shipbuilding, breweries and builders.

Tertiary
Businesses in the tertiary sector provide a service, an intangible product. The service is provided by people who have been trained to offer it. Examples include fitness instructors, hotels, supermarkets, hairdressers and health care providers.

Quaternary
This is the newest sector of industry. Businesses in the quaternary sector provide a knowledge-based and information service and are often concerned with innovation, research and development. This includes consultancy, ICT and computing, education,

scientific research and financial services. People working in the quaternary sector are highly skilled.

Trends

Each country tends to move from one sector to the next after a period of time; the United Kingdom is a good example. In industrialised countries, the tertiary and quaternary sectors now account for most of the business activity that takes place. Primary and secondary industries no longer have such a major role in these countries but there is still some evidence of these activities taking place, even in Scotland. For example, a significant amount of oil and gas extraction still takes place off the coast of Aberdeen and shipbuilding still takes place on the Clyde in Glasgow.

⚠ Watch point

Businesses can belong to more than one sector of industry.

GO! Paired activity

Do some research to find out:

1. The proportion of businesses in each sector of industry in the UK today.
2. Reasons why the UK has moved from one sector to another.

Present your results in a poster and include a graph showing your answer to Q1. Make sure your graph is labelled appropriately. For Q2, try to analyse and interpret as best you can the reasons you find. Your Teacher/Lecturer will help you with this.

🌳 Skills

- Research
- ICT
- Thinking

Wealth creation

Wealth is created by a business by adding value to a product as it goes through the production process. Let's recap this process from National 5: when jeans are being made, they go through the following chain of production:

Cotton is cleaned thoroughly

Indigo is used to turn the cotton blue

The cotton is weaved together into denim

Parts of the jeans are cut out of the denim using templates

Workers sew the parts of the jeans together

The jeans are stone washed to make them look worn

The jeans are pressed

As the jeans move from one stage of production to another, **wealth is being created**.

This is because **value is being added** to the price that will be charged by the business for the product.

Think about it ... the jeans are worth more as a finished product rather than all the raw materials (cotton, indigo, buttons, zip etc) sitting in a pile themselves. Another example would be building a house; as the house is built it is worth more than the bricks, wood and paint sitting on an empty piece of land doing nothing.

When we add up the final value of all goods and services provided in the UK, we have a figure known as the **gross domestic product (GDP)**. At Higher level, we need to consider the impact that the process of creating wealth has on the UK economy.

Benefits	Costs
• Jobs are created and therefore this reduces the UK's unemployment figure • When people become employed, they might have access to training and the opportunity to learn new skills • As a result of less unemployment, demand for goods and services increases and the standard of living increases • Tax is paid by businesses and individuals when they have a job and this money is paid to the Government who can then invest this money into different Government services, eg health, police and education • Other businesses will be keen to invest • Infrastructure (eg access to utilities such as water and electricity) can be improved, as can roads and transport links	• Businesses can have a large environmental impact on a country or specific location (eg noise and traffic pollution and an increase in wastage) • The volume of non-renewable resources, eg oil, can decrease • Greenfield sites (land that has previously been unused or used for agriculture) are lost – however, this could be seen as an advantage • Too much demand for goods and services can cause inflation; this is when the price of goods and services rises and may mean people can no longer afford to purchase some products

GO! Group activity

Think of a project happening in your local area (eg a new business being built). Prepare a brief presentation on this project. Your presentation should include:

1. A brief introduction to the project you have chosen and why.
2. Some background information on the project.
3. Why the project is taking place.
4. The benefits of the project to the economy and environment.
5. The costs of the project to the economy and environment.
6. A conclusion, with reasons, stating why your group thinks the project will benefit the local area or not.

Be prepared to evaluate your presentation once you have delivered it. Note down any improvements you could make next time in your learning journal, and what you could have done to improve your own contribution.

Skills

- Decision-making
- Thinking
- Research
- Communication

UNEMPLOYED

Make the link

Environmental issues are explored in various chapters in these Course Notes.

⚠ Watch point

Keep up-to-date with what is happening in the economy in the TV/radio news and in good quality newspapers. Ask your Teacher/Lecturer for more information about the features of good quality newspapers.

GO! Individual activity

The Commonwealth Games took place in Glasgow in 2014. This had a positive and negative impact on Glasgow and, in particular, the specific locations in which events took place. Your task is to do some research and find out:

1. The number of jobs the Games created, both during construction and while the games took place, and the benefits of this job creation.
2. The facilities that the Games have provided for the people of Glasgow and the benefits of these new facilities.
3. The number of people who visited Glasgow for the games and the benefits of this on the local economy.
4. Examples of the negative impact the Games have had on the local community and Glasgow, and the extent of that impact.

When you are completing this task, really try to think about (analyse) the consequences of what you are finding out. Be prepared to discuss your findings with the rest of your class. Your Teacher/Lecturer will collate a detailed analysis of all the findings of the class.

Skills

-   Thinking
-   Research
-   Communication

Questions

1. Describe the four sectors of industry.
2. Define the term 'wealth creation'.
3. Define the term 'gross domestic product'.
4. Suggest three advantages and three disadvantages of creating wealth for the UK.

Types of business organisations

A business belongs to one sector of the economy. At National 5, the focus was on small to medium sized organisations, whereas at Higher, the focus is on large organisations. A large organisation is one that employs more than 250 people.

At National 5 the following types of businesses were explored:

⚙: Make the link

Make sure you revise what you learned at National 5 about types of businesses.

💡 Revision Activity

Download and complete revision sheet 1 from the Leckie & Leckie website. This looks at types of businesses.

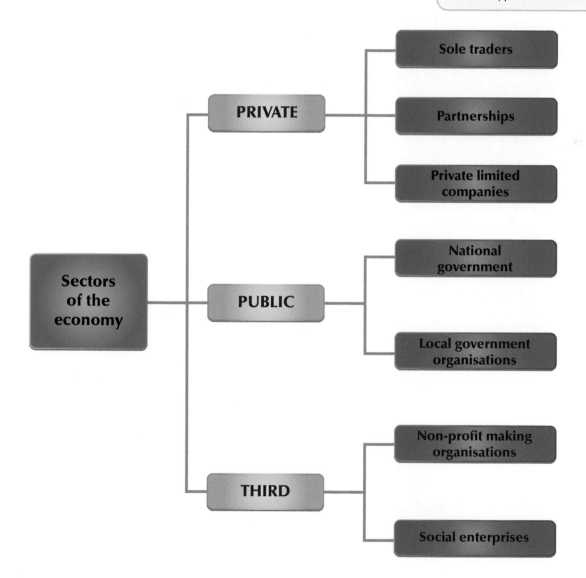

At Higher level, you need to be able to compare the features of the following large organisations:

Private Sector	Public Sector	Third Sector
• Public limited companies • Franchises • Multinationals	• National government organisations and agencies	• Non-profit making organisations, eg charities • Social enterprises

⚠ Watch point

Sectors of the economy are different from sectors of industry.

⚠ Watch point

When comparing different types of businesses, think about: who owns them, who controls them and how they are financed.

Public limited companies

A public limited company (plc) is a company that is owned by shareholders. Shareholders are people who have bought shares in the company, perhaps through the London Stock Exchange. The company is owned by shareholders and run by a Board of Directors who have been appointed on behalf of shareholders to control and manage the company.

Advantages

- Limited liability for the shareholders of the company (this means if the company was to go bankrupt, shareholders would only lose the money they invested into the company and not their own personal assets). This also means that shareholders are maybe more likely to invest in the company.

- Large amounts of capital (finance) can be raised by selling more shares via the stock exchange and lenders may feel more confident in investing in larger companies.

- Can often take advantage of economies of scale because of their size. This means they can obtain discounts for buying, eg raw materials in bulk.

- Plcs can control more of the market compared to smaller organisations and therefore have more power within it.

Disadvantages

- Financial statements have to be published annually, which will involve a cost to produce them.

- There is no control over who can buy shares in the company.

- The company has to abide by the Companies Act to avoid legal action being taken.

- Profits may be lower when the company is initially set up due to high start-up costs.

Franchises

Ever fancied having your own McDonalds restaurant? Well, you can, by opening a franchise. A person who starts a business and provides a product or service supplied by another business (the **franchisor**) is known as a **franchisee** and operates a business known as a **franchise**. The franchisee is allowed to use the business name (eg McDonalds) and sell its products.

There are advantages and disadvantages of franchising to both the **franchisee** and **franchisor**.

Franchisee:

Advantages	Disadvantages
• They can set up a business using a business name that is well established and that people are familiar with. This could allow them to gain customers and sales quickly compared to setting up a brand new business. It also reduces the risk of failure. • Advertising costs are paid for by the franchisor which saves the franchisee having to spend money on this themselves. • Franchisor carries out training for the whole business and therefore it is appropriate to the needs of the workforce and will save the franchisee money.	• It requires a considerable sum of money to set up a franchise and the franchisee may not have this money available. • The franchisee might have little or no control over the products available, their price or the layout of the store. The franchisee might find this frustrating as they cannot inject any new ideas into the business. • Some of the profit earned has to be given to the franchisor, thereby reducing the money that the franchisee earns.

Franchisor:

Advantages	Disadvantages
• Income is guaranteed as the franchisee normally pays a percentage of profit each year to the franchisor. • If the business does not work, the cost of failure is split and therefore risk is shared. • Market share of the whole franchise increases as more branches are being opened.	• As only a percentage of turnover is given to the franchisor by the franchisee, this might be lower than what the franchisor could have earned themselves. • A franchisee could damage the reputation and image of the business and this could cause problems for the whole franchise.

Multinationals

A multinational organisation is one that operates in more than one country. It will normally have a headquarters based in one country; this is known as the 'home' country. Because it operates in more than one country, it will be globally recognised. A socially responsible multinational organisation may have a positive impact on the local economy and community by providing jobs and creating wealth for the local area.

Advantages

- Economies of scale can be taken advantage of, therefore reducing costs.

- Legal restrictions can be avoided in other countries compared to the home country.

- May be able to take advantage of different tax regulations in other countries, therefore increasing profitability.

- Expanding abroad will mean the organisation becomes bigger, increasing sales, and also safer from takeovers by other organisations.

- Government grants that do not require to be paid back might be given in some countries for locating there.

- Resources, eg labour, might be cheaper in some countries, reducing the overall expenses.

Disadvantages

- Each country's laws need to be complied with, which might mean changes need to be made to the goods or service, and these might be expensive.

- The culture might vary from one country to another and the organisation will need to consider this.

- Language barriers may make trading more difficult and expensive if language interpreters need to be employed.

- Language barriers may also mean that communication is misinterpreted and decisions wrongly made.

National government organisations

Public sector organisations are owned by the Government on behalf of the taxpayer and aim to provide a service to the general public. They are funded by taxes that individuals and businesses have to pay. Different types of taxes exist including income tax, road tax and council tax.

The UK Parliament consists of three components: the Monarch, the House of Lords and the House of Commons. The House of Commons, based in London, has major responsibility for what happens in the UK. It aims to debate and take action on issues such as defence, taxation, the economy and laws. Different political parties (politicians with similar values) compete with each other to win control of the House of Commons. Examples of political parties include Labour, the Conservatives and the Liberal Democrats, but there are more. The House of Commons has Members of Parliament (MPs) who are elected by the public. MPs report to the House of Lords, who in turn report to the Monarch.

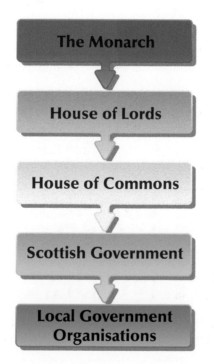

Different national agencies exist to support the work of the Government. They provide a service, are owned by the taxpayer and are funded by taxes. Some examples include:

- HM Revenue & Customs
- Royal Mint
- Office of Fair Trading

Scottish Government

The Scottish Government has delegated responsibility from the UK Parliament for issues such as education, health and transport. It is run by Members of the Scottish Parliament (MSPs), who are elected by the Scottish public.

Local government organisations

Local government organisations (or local authorities) get funding from the Scottish Government to deliver specific services in a specific area of Scotland. These include running schools, providing leisure facilities and emptying our rubbish bins!

GO! Paired activity

The structure of the public sector can be confusing. As an expert, you are required to prepare an information sheet on the structure of the public sector in the UK. You should do considerable research, using good quality sources, to put together an information sheet. Your information sheet should include:

- A detailed description of the structure of the UK public sector (national, Scottish and local government).
- Information about the three components of Parliament.
- A description of the purpose and responsibilities of any three national agencies.

You will find the UK Parliament and Direct Gov's websites useful resources.

Scan these QR codes for the UK Parliament website (1st code) and for Direct Gov's website (2nd code).

Third sector

Non-profit making organisations such as charities and voluntary organisations are set up to support specific causes.

Charities are owned and controlled by a Board of Trustees. They are regulated by the Government, and the income they make is put towards a specific cause. Charities will undertake fundraising activities to raise finance, eg by asking for grants/donations through TV appeals, street collections or by selling unwanted items in a charity shop.

Voluntary organisations such as community football clubs or youth clubs aim to provide a service to people, but without the profit-making motive. A committee is normally set up to manage the voluntary organisation and people will volunteer to undertake specific duties, eg Chairperson, Secretary etc. Most voluntary organisations will ask for donations as well as holding fundraising events, eg fun days and sponsored events, to raise finance.

Social enterprises

Social enterprises have a social or environmental aim rather than to make profit for owners or shareholders, but are run in a business-like way. The business will let customers know what the social enterprise is trying to do and who it is trying to help. At least half of the profit that it makes, through selling goods and services, must be invested into meeting the aim of the social enterprise. Unlike some charities, they don't rely on grants and donations, but some social enterprises do become charities. The main difference between a social enterprise and a charity is its legal structure and the fact that social enterprises have less regulation by the Government.

Examples of social enterprises

- **Aberdeen Foyer** – a social enterprise set up to try and help homeless youths in the Aberdeenshire area. As well as this, they provide opportunities for young people to develop employability and life skills. The opportunities they provide range from construction and property maintenance to graphic design and driving training.

- **Active4All** – this social enterprise provides nearly 100 jobs by collecting waste materials and unwanted furniture and then selling them. It is based in Glasgow.

- **Wooden Spoon Catering** – a social enterprise based in Dundee with the aim of providing job and education opportunities for women who might be isolated or in a vulnerable position.

> ⚠ **Watch point**
>
> A social enterprise is different from a private sector business that operates in an ethical or socially responsible way.

GO! Class activity

Arrange a visit to a local social enterprise or invite a speaker from a local social enterprise along to talk to your class.
Try to find out as much as you can about how the social enterprise works, what it does and the benefits that it brings.

♆ Skills

- Communication
- Thinking

Social Enterprise Scotland

Just Enterprise

Social Enterprise UK

100 Social Enterprises

GO! Further reading

Further information on social enterprises can be found by scanning the QR codes opposite or by using the following websites:
Social Enterprise Scotland -
http://www.socialenterprisescotland.org.uk/
Just Enterprise - http://www.justenterprise.org/
Social Enterprise UK - http://www.socialenterprise.org.uk/
A list of the top 100 Social Enterprises -
http://se100.net/index/

♆ Skills

- Research
- ICT

? Questions

1. Compare a private limited company and a public limited company.
2. Describe two advantages and two disadvantages of a public limited company.
3. Define the term 'franchise'.
4. Suggest two advantages and two disadvantages of franchising for the franchisor.
5. Suggest two advantages and two disadvantages of franchising for the franchisee.
6. Suggest two advantages and two disadvantages of being a multinational.
7. Suggest how a multinational may be socially responsible.
8. What consequences might the following have for a multinational?

   - Language differences
   - Cultural differences
   - Cheaper labour
   - Different tax rates
   - Easier access to raw materials

9. Compare local and national government.
10. Describe the different organisations operating in the third sector.

Objectives

An **objective** is a goal or a target that a business has. They provide a focus for the organisation and its workforce to work towards over a period of time. They are important because they can be used to measure how successful an organisation is. An organisation will usually make its objectives public, eg in its mission statement and on its website.

A **mission statement** sets out the vision and aims of an organisation. It lets different stakeholders (see page 66) see what the organisation will do in the future and what it might mean for them:

- It will tell employees what it plans to do and they can think about how this would impact their own job.

- Prospective employees might use it to see whether their own values match those of the organisation and whether or not they would fit in.

- It can be used to inform customers about future plans the organisation has.

- It can be used to raise the profile and image of the organisation and might attract media attention and, in the long run, potentially increase sales.

A number of objectives were explored at National 5. However, at Higher level, it is necessary to be able to justify why an objective is important, as well as learning about other objectives.

> **⚠ Watch point**
> Different types of businesses will have different objectives.

> **⁘ Make the link**
> Make sure you revise what you learned at National 5 about different objectives.

> **⚠ Watch point**
> Make sure you can say why an objective is important for a business.

Objective	What is it?	Why is it important?
Survival	To continue trading; to exist	Other objectives would be pointless if the business did not exist.
Profit	To have more income (eg through sales) than costs.	Most private sector businesses have this aim. Dividend payments to shareholders in a plc will be based on profit.
Customer Satisfaction	To make customers happy.	To ensure customer loyalty and to encourage new customers.
Market Leader	To become the biggest business in a market.	This will highlight the fact that the business has the greatest number of customers compared to competitors.

Other objectives that we need to learn about at Higher are:

- Corporate social responsibility
- Satisficing
- Managerial objectives
- Growth

Corporate social responsibility

Corporate social responsibility (CSR) might be known as social responsibility or ethics. An organisation with this aim will behave in a responsible way; this might involve treating suppliers fairly and/or protecting the environment. Large organisations may have a code of conduct or a set of regulations that must be complied with if working with that organisation (eg a code of conduct on what it expects from its suppliers).

There are many different ways an organisation can be socially responsible:

- Making sure raw materials come from sustainable sources (sources that can be replaced), eg trees when paper is being manufactured (see page 165).

- Trying to reduce its carbon footprint as much as possible, eg using the most environmentally friendly method of distribution (see page 144).

- Making sure suppliers are paid fairly for what they produce, eg by adopting a fair trade policy (see page 165).

- Recycling as much as possible (see page 165).

- Providing opportunities for employees to participate in physical activity and promoting healthy eating, eg providing cycling facilities to get to work or providing healthy options in the canteen.

This objective is becoming more important in a modern world; people expect businesses to behave responsibly and, if they don't, this will impact negatively on their image and customers would likely shop elsewhere. While acting in a socially responsible way might be costly in the short-term for an organisation, the long-term benefits of adopting this aim will far outweigh the costs and potential consequences of not doing so!

Make the link

Fair trade (page 165) is also relevant when exploring social responsibility.

Case study

PRIMARK®

Primark aims to provide affordable and fashionable clothes to its customers and has placed a strong focus on social responsibility. It has three core values that summarise its commitment to social responsibility:

Primark has a code of conduct that sets out the minimum standards expected from its suppliers and from people working in its factories. These standards include:

- Employment must be entered into freely (ie there is no 'forced' employment and no child labour).

- Providing a safe, clean and hygienic working environment.

- There will be no discrimination.

- People will be treated in a humane way.

- Hours of work will not be excessive.

Primark
Ethical trading

Primark conducts regular visits to its suppliers to ensure standards are being maintained and its code of conduct is being complied with. Further information about Primark and its commitment to social responsibility can be found by scanning the QR code opposite or on the Primark ethical trading website (https://www.primark.com/en/our-ethics).

Questions

1. What is social responsibility?
2. What aim does Primark have?
3. Why does it have three core values?
4. What are its three core values?
5. What is a code of conduct?
6. How does Primark ensure its code of conduct is being followed?
7. Suggest a disadvantage of Primark having a code of conduct.

GO! Paired activity

You are going to find out more about an organisation and its commitment to social responsibility.

1. Choose an organisation.
2. Do some research to find out about its commitment to social responsibility.

- What does its mission statement say about social responsibility?
- Does it have a policy or code of conduct?
- What does it expect of its stakeholders?
- What does it do to behave ethically?
- How does it make sure that social responsibility is being implemented?

Summarise your findings in a poster, short presentation or in a discussion forum. Be prepared to share these with the rest of your class.

Skills

- Research
- Thinking
- Communication
- Decision-making

GO! Group or class discussion

Find some examples of an organisation that has been criticised in the media for not being socially responsible.

- What did the organisation do?
- What consequences or possible consequences has it had for the organisation?
- What recommendations do you have for the organisation to avoid this situation in the future?
- What would the costs and benefits of these recommendations be?

Summarise your findings in a poster, short presentation or in a discussion forum. Be prepared to share these with the rest of your class.

Skills

- Research
- Thinking
- Enterprise
- Communication
- Decision-making

Satisficing

This means aiming for a satisfactory position, ie 'it is good enough'. It is based on the idea of Herbert Simon, a famous economist. It might not be the ideal situation or solution but it will be adequate. Sometimes it is not possible to aim for the ideal situation or solution, particularly in the short-term, because of the costs involved or because of external factors (eg an uncertain economy or legislation) that might prevent the ideal being achieved.

Make the link

External factors are covered on pages 59–65.

Managerial objectives

Managers might have their own internal objectives. They might want to receive bonuses for achieving certain targets or other fringe benefits ('perks') such as a company car. These objectives can be motivating to a manager but they might put their own objectives before the organisation's.

Growth

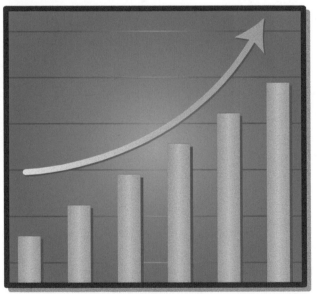

Businesses might aim to grow for a number of reasons:

- To increase sales and profit which in turn will increase the return on investment for owners (eg dividends for shareholders).

- To increase the number of customers which will increase profits and market share, and may enable the organisation to become a marker leader.

- To take advantage of economies of scale (discounts for bulk buying), thereby reducing costs.

- To reduce the risk of a takeover by another organisation.

- To gain a better reputation in the marketplace which will encourage new customers to buy, thereby increasing sales and ultimately profit.

Businesses can grow in a number of ways. The diagram below shows you some of the different methods of growth.

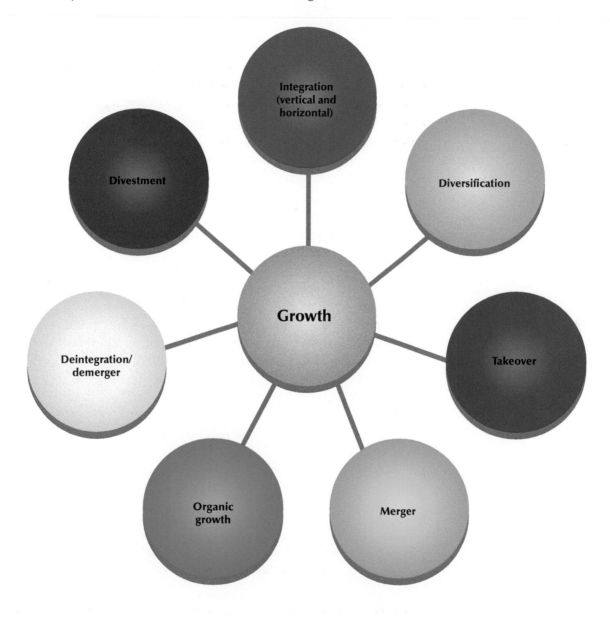

Integration

Horizontal integration – two businesses providing the same service, or producing the same product, join together (eg two airlines joining together). This will cause the business to become bigger, gain a greater market share and will reduce the number of competitors in the market. As a result of fewer competitors, higher prices could be charged by the business. It also allows the business to gain economies of scale, which will in turn lower production costs and increase profit.

When businesses in the same industry, but who operate at different stages of production, join together this is called **vertical integration**. This cuts out the middle-men involved with two separate businesses, and therefore cuts costs. There are two types of vertical integration.

Backward vertical integration – taking over a supplier, eg a jeans manufacturer taking over a cotton farmer. By taking over a supplier it means that the business should have sufficient supplies available at reasonable prices, as they will not need to add the element of profit to raw materials.

Forward vertical integration – taking over a customer, eg a jeans manufacturer taking over a jeans shop. By taking over a customer this will mean that supplies are readily available to the shop, helping to ensure regular sales.

Diversification

Diversification is when two businesses that provide different goods and services join together. It is also referred to as a **conglomerate**. It will reduce the risk of failure by operating in more than one market and will also allow profit to be obtained from more than one market. Diversification can also occur when one business decides to begin trading in a new market, eg a supermarket deciding to open an optician or pharmacy. This also reduces risk and allows for increased profits.

Takeover

A takeover is when one large business takes control and ownership of a smaller business.

Merger

A merger is when two businesses of approximately the same size agree to become one. This will allow sales and market share to increase.

Organic growth

Organic growth happens when the business increases the number of goods and services it offers or increases the number of branches/outlets and employees that it has. This will help to increase sales and profit.

Deintegration/Demerger

Deintegration (or demerger) occurs when a business splits into two or more separate businesses. It will allow new organisations to focus their resources on core activity and become more efficient, therefore cutting costs.

Divestment

Divestment is when a business sells off some of its assets or smaller parts of the business to raise finance. The parts of the business that are sold off are normally less profitable and this finance can be put back into the business.

🔍 Case study

The International Airlines Group (IAG)

British Airways and Iberia merged in November 2011 to create one of Europe's biggest airlines. It is now part of the International Airlines Group (IAG). Both airlines continue to market and operate as single entities under the IAG umbrella, but believe there are many benefits to the customer of this merger:

- A greater choice of destinations for travellers.

- A greater number of flight times.

- A greater number of executive lounges for travellers.

- Greater rewards through the frequent flyer programme.

? Questions

1. Suggest three reasons why businesses such as British Airways and Iberia would want to grow.
2. What is a merger?
3. What type of integration is a merger?
4. Suggest three advantages to a business of a merger.

Case study

Morrisons

Morrisons began as a market stall in Bradford, England, and is now one of the UK's biggest supermarket chains. It currently has a 12% share of the supermarket market. It employs around 129,000 people in its supermarkets as well as in other parts of its business. It has over 150,000 trolleys in its supermarkets!

MORRISONS
More of what matters

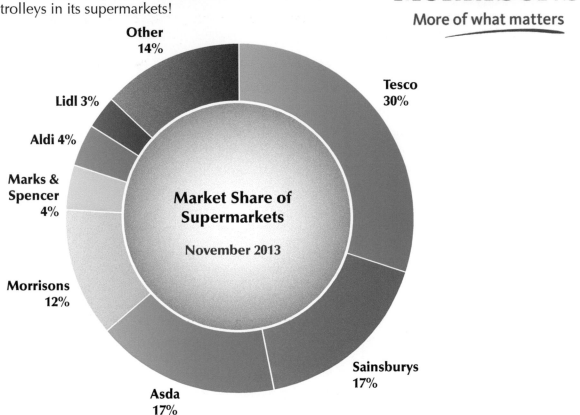

Source: Kantar Worldpanel and Marks & Spencer

The source of Morrisons' food has always been a key concern. It sources a lot of its food from its own suppliers (eg farms for meat) and believes that this allows it to offer better promotions to its customers and, at the same time, support the growth of profitability. It has added to this by purchasing Flower World in 2011 to enable it to grow and sell fresh flowers in its stores.

The changing business environment has meant that Morrisons is keen to keep up-to-date with what customers demand and has recently invested money in the convenience market. It has just bought over 60 stores from other retailers to expand its range of local convenience stores, and hopes to have over 100 of these open during 2014. It is growing its online presence by purchasing Kiddicare, an online business supplying baby and infant merchandise, as well as launching Morrisons Cellar.

Morrisons strongly believes in operating ethically throughout all of its business operations, and is committed to reducing waste through its 'Great Taste, Less Waste' scheme. It works closely with its local communities to support various projects and initiatives, including educational projects for schools and charity partnerships.

? Questions

1.   Define the following terms: 'market share' and 'market growth'.
2.   Explain the reasons why Morrisons wants to grow.
3.   Morrisons has grown in a number of ways. Describe three methods of growth given in the case study.
4.   Suggest two advantages and two disadvantages of each method of growth given in Q3.
5.   Identify four ways Morrisons is demonstrating its commitment to social responsibility.
6.   Suggest reasons why Morrisons wants to be seen as socially responsible.

GO! Paired or group activity

Research an example of a business that has grown.

- Describe the method of growth used.
- What advantages does this have for the business?
- What implications does it have for the business?
- What criticism does the business receive in the media about this growth? Why?
- What could the business do to prevent media criticism?

Summarise your findings in a poster, short presentation or in a discussion forum. Be prepared to share these with the rest of your class.

Skills

- Research
- Communication
- Thinking
- Enterprise

? Questions

1.   For each sector of business, describe objectives that businesses in that sector would have.
2.   For each objective given in Q1, give a reason why this objective would be important.
3.   Describe methods of growth that might be used by a multinational.
4.   Justify the use of diversification as a method of growth.
5.   Justify the use of divestment as a method of growth.
6.   Suggest a consequence of managerial objectives.
7.   Suggest two reasons why customer satisfaction may be an objective.

Internal structure

An organisation consists of a group of people who come together for a common goal or aim. They organise themselves internally to suit the type of activities that the organisation is carrying out.

Organisations can group themselves in a number of different ways. This depends on several factors:

- Size of the organisation (larger organisations tend to require a more formal structure compared to smaller ones).

- The technology being used (this could be used to communicate with other parts of the organisation in other locations).

- Who the customer is (in other words, the target market).

- The good or service that is being provided.

- The amount of finance available to the organisation (this might limit the type of structure or grouping that could be used).

An organisation chart shows how an organisation is structured. It shows:

- Who has overall **responsibility** for the organisation.

- The different levels of **authority** and **responsibility** within the organisation.

- The lines of **communication** and the **chain of command**.

- The **span of control** for different managers.

- Different **relationships** that exist within the organisation.

- Where work could be **delegated** to **subordinates**.

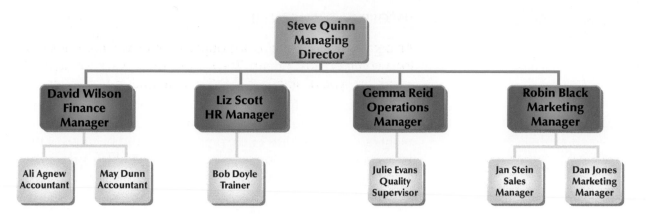

The organisation structure shows the formal lines of communication that take place and the route that is taken for information and instructions to reach a particular place. Despite the existence of **formal structures** (such as the one above), **informal structures** can sometimes exist. Informal structures exist when communication takes place in ways that the organisation structure does not show.

There are a number of key terms that you need to learn about when you are analysing how organisations are structured.

- **Responsibility** – being answerable for decisions and actions taken within the organisation.

- **Authority** – having power to make decisions.

- **Chain of command** - this shows how instructions are passed down through an organisation and how communication can flow up and down the organisation. A long chain of command may mean that communication and decision-making is slower compared to a short chain of command. Decisions might therefore be slower to implement.

- **Delegation** – giving the authority and responsibility to someone else to carry out a particular task (eg a manager giving the authority and responsibility to a subordinate to carry out a task).

Grouping of activities

Organisations can group their activities in a number of different ways. The factors that influence the type of grouping to be chosen are given on page 36.

Functional grouping

Functional grouping means grouping by department, and people working in these departments have a similar area of interest. These functions might include: Human Resources (HR),

Make the link

These Course Notes explore different functional activities in Chapters 4-7.

Make the link

External factors are explored on pages 59–65.

Operations, Marketing, Finance and Research & Development. People can contact specific departments if they require specialist advice or help (eg Marketing might contact HR when recruiting a new employee for that department). Clear lines of authority exist (as shown on the organisation chart) between subordinates and managers, and everyone will usually have clearly defined tasks and duties to carry out. Sometimes departmental aims might overtake the aims of the organisation and because of this, the organisation can sometimes find it difficult to respond to changing market conditions and external factors.

Product grouping

This type of grouping exists when the organisation is structured around the products that it sells. Each department in the organisation concentrates on one specific product, which results in specialist knowledge of each product within that department. Each department is also able to respond quickly to changes in the market, but if their product is not performing well, this is easily identifiable to managers. If the organisation introduces a new product, new employees need to be employed. There may also be rivalry between different departments that can be counterproductive to working relationships within the organisation. Line relationships (who an employee reports to) in product groupings may not be as clear as more traditional, functional structures.

This is an example of a product grouping:

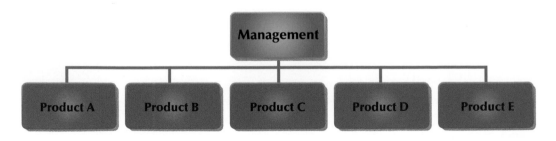

Customer grouping

This is grouping by customer types (in other words, grouping by market segment or target market). Products can be marketed towards each specific customer group. The organisation can build up loyalty with their customers because activities are focused on the specific customer group, and therefore a higher level of customer service is achieved. High staffing costs can be a disadvantage of this type of structure.

Make the link

Customer satisfaction was explored in National 5 Business Management.

The following structure shows a customer grouping for a holiday company:

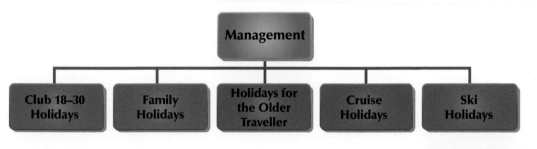

Location/Geographical grouping

This type of grouping exists when the organisation is structured around specific locations. The needs of customers within each specific location can be focused on and the organisation can become familiar with different cultures that exist in different locations. Technology can be used to communicate with staff in different locations (eg videoconferencing), though this can be expensive. Duplication of resources can be a downside to this structure.

⚠ **Watch point**

Make sure you can describe different types of structures as well as give reasons for why they would be used.

The following structure shows a location/geographical grouping for a UK based company:

ⓖⓞ! Individual activity

Create a mindmap with the different types of organisational groupings. Give a description of each and include some advantages and disadvantages. Make your mindmap more attractive by including relevant diagrams. You can use appropriate software packages to help if you prefer.
Keep a copy of your mindmap as a revision tool.

♀ Skills

- ICT
- Thinking

❓Questions

1. Describe the influences on the choice of its structure that an organisation may have.
2. Describe the content of an organisation chart.
3. Define the following terms:

   - Delegation
   - Chain of command
   - Authority
   - Responsibility

4. Name different functional areas that might exist within an organisation.
5. Compare two methods of activity grouping.
6. Suggest two advantages of a geographical structure.
7. Suggest two advantages of a functional structure.
8. Justify the use of a customer grouping.

Span of control

This is the number of subordinates (people) who report to one person. For example, a manager might have five people who report to them so they therefore have five subordinates.

A wide span of control will mean that many people report to one person whereas a narrow span of control will mean that very few people report to one person.

Wide span of control

- More empowerment is possible due to the number of subordinates.

- Tasks can be delegated more easily to the subordinate most suitably skilled to carry these out, however, employees may feel reluctant and uncomfortable with this.

- As there are a large number of subordinates, this can cause extra stress for the manager who may have little time to deal with staff-related issues.

- Managers may feel that, as they have more subordinates to manage, they are more powerful and this can be motivating to them.

- The organisation will have fewer managers and therefore saves money.

- A shorter chain of command will exist and therefore communication and decision-making is likely to be more effective.

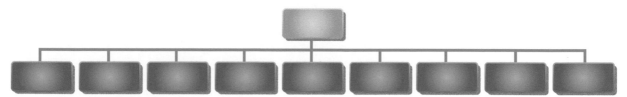

Narrow span of control

- Less empowerment as there are fewer subordinates to manage and the manager is unlikely to delegate as much.

- Delegation may be more difficult as there are fewer subordinates.

- Subordinates have more opportunities to communicate and interact with their manager.

- Subordinates are more likely to have the chance to participate in decision-making and planning.

- A long chain of command will exist and therefore communication and decision-making might be slower.

Organisation structures

Tall and flat structures

A **tall**, or hierarchical, structure has many layers of management. This means that it has a long chain of command; it will take time for instructions and information to pass through the structure. These structures are often found in public sector organisations but, as a consequence of the global economic downturn in the early 2000s, many public sector organisations have restructured to save staffing costs. (Changing structure is covered on pages 45–46).

Flat structures contain fewer layers of management compared to tall ones. This means that flat structures have a shorter chain of command; it will take less time for instructions and information to pass through the structure. This type of structure is often found in smaller organisations. Because there are fewer layers of management compared to tall structures, the cost of management salaries will be less.

Matrix structures

Matrix (or project-based) structures tend to be formed when a specific task or project is to be carried out. People from across the organisation will come together from various departments to form the matrix structure. When the task or project has been completed, the matrix structure will become obsolete. A project or team leader will be appointed to provide leadership to the task or project being undertaken. Because people from across the organisation may participate in this structure, it can be motivating for employees and useful to the organisation when problems are

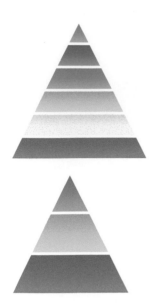

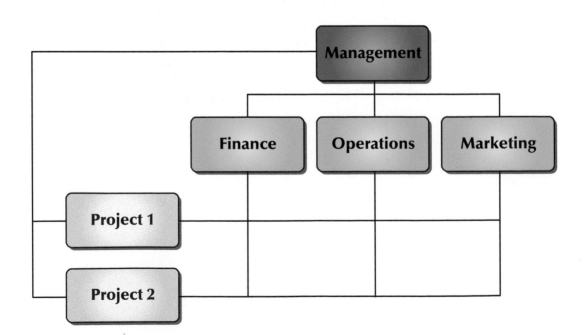

being solved. Even though it gives employees the opportunity to learn new skills, by participating in a project or task, it can be costly to implement and for the organisation to coordinate. Employees may find having two managers (eg from their own functional area as well as for the matrix structure) confusing.

Entrepreneurial structures

An **entrepreneurial structure** is often found in smaller organisations. This type of structure is seen when decisions are made by the owner or certain managers with very little input (if anything) from employees. Even though it means decisions can be made quickly, because employees are not involved in the process, it can reduce employees' motivation. It also means that good ideas or creative solutions to problems are not considered because employees have not been consulted. This type of structure is not often found in larger organisations because it would place too much of a heavy workload on managers who have to make decisions.

Centralisation and decentralisation

In a **centralised structure**, decisions are made by the senior management of the organisation. This structure is often associated with tall (hierarchical) structures. In a plc, for example, decisions might be made by managers at the head office rather than managers in different branches. Employees at various levels of the hierarchy are not consulted about decisions being made which can result in them becoming demotivated.

In a **decentralised structure**, decision-making is delegated to departments and subordinates. This type of structure is associated with a flat structure and because people at different levels of the hierarchy are involved in decision-making, it can motivate them. Because decisions are made by different departments, it can be harder to ensure consistency across the organisation (eg departments might make decisions to suit their own needs rather than those of the whole organisation) whereas a centralised structure would achieve this consistency.

Relationships within organisations

Different types of relationships exist between people in organisations.

Line Relationships	This is a relationship between a subordinate and their line manager *eg Steve Quinn and David Wilson on the chart shown on page 37.*
Lateral Relationships	This is a relationship between two or more people on the same level of the organisation *eg Liz Scott and Gemma Reid on the chart shown on page 37.*
Functional Relationships	This is a relationship between two functional areas in an organisation, eg one providing support to another. *An example is Human Resources providing advice to the Marketing department when recruiting a new member of staff.*
Staff Relationships	This is a relationship between two or more people in an organisation who provide advice or support to others.
Informal Relationships	An informal relationship exists when two or more people communicate on an informal basis, normally outwith the organisation *eg two people meeting for coffee after work.*

? Questions

1. Compare a wide and narrow span of control.
2. What implications might a wide span of control have for an organisation?
3. Discuss the impact that a narrow span of control might have on decision-making.
4. Compare a tall and a flat structure.
5. Describe five characteristics of a matrix structure.
6. Suggest advantages and disadvantages of an entrepreneurial structure.
7. Compare a centralised and decentralised structure.
8. Describe advantages and disadvantages of a centralised and decentralised structure.
9. Describe types of relationships that can exist in an organisation.
10. Compare a formal and informal relationship.

Changing structure

An organisation might decide to change its structure. It may do this because:

- The size of the organisation has changed.
- The availability of finance has changed.
- Market conditions have changed.
- New technology has become available.

The managers of an organisation may decide to change its structure to ensure that it continues to meet the aims and objectives it has set itself.

An organisation may decide to change its structure by **delayering** or **downsizing**.

Delayering

Delayering means removing layers of management from the structure. For example, moving from a tall structure to a flat structure. As well as saving money on management salaries, it allows for quicker communication and decision-making because there are fewer layers. Market conditions may be responded to more quickly compared to in a taller structure. Employees may feel more empowered to make decisions and to use their own initiative; this can increase motivation and productivity. This is because managers will have a wider span of control and ultimately might mean that the supervision and management of employees could be more difficult. Delayering also means that there will be fewer promotion opportunities for existing staff.

> **⚠ Watch point**
> Make sure you clearly understand the difference between **delayering** and **downsizing**.

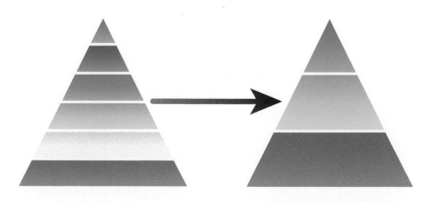

Downsizing

Downsizing involves removing some of the activities that the organisation carries out from its structure. For example, closing a branch, factory or division in response to external factors.

Some activities might be **outsourced** to enable the organisation to concentrate on its core activities. The organisation carrying out the activity on behalf of the organisation that is downsizing will be paid for doing this, which could be expensive. It also means that the organisation needs to trust the outsourced organisation to deliver on time and to the standard expected. Effective communication between the two organisations is crucial to the success of outsourcing.

? Questions

1. Suggest reasons why an organisation may wish to change structure.
2. Compare delayering and downsizing.
3. Justify the use of delayering.
4. Discuss the impact of delayering on existing staff.
5. Suggest reasons why an organisation may outsource.

★ Key questions

1. Compare features of two business organisations from different sectors of the economy. In your answer, refer to:

    *   ownership
    *   control
    *   finance

2. Describe and justify an objective for three different types of business organisations.
3. Describe and justify three types of internal structures that a business could adopt.

Summary

This chapter provided you with an overview of the role, activities and objectives of different types of businesses and different types of internal structures.

The learning intentions for this chapter were:

*   The role of business in society
*   Types of business organisations
*   Objectives
*   Internal structures

By successfully answering the key questions, you will have proved that you have grasped the main topics covered in this chapter.

3 Business Environment

⚠ Watch point

You must be able to describe the impact each internal factor will have, ie the consequence of it on the business.

Internal factors

Internal factors are things within the business that impact upon how it operates.

- **Financial** – there might not be enough finance to make new purchases. This might mean that raw materials cannot be purchased and production stops. If production stops, orders might be delayed and customers become unhappy. A lack of finance might also mean that objectives, eg growth, cannot be met.

- **Employees** – employees might not have the correct skills or motivation required to carry out a task. If they don't have the correct skills, the quality of their work might be poor, which results in a product of poor quality. Customers are likely to be put off if a product is of poor quality. If the motivation of employees is low (ie they don't want to work as hard as they could), their productivity will be low and deadlines might be missed. Low motivation could also result in a higher absence rate.

- **Management** – managers might not have enough experience or skill in decision-making. This could result in poor decisions being made that impact upon the whole organisation, eg fewer sales.

- **Existing technology** – the technology that a business has might not be the best available or suitable to carry out certain tasks. If technology is out of date, the production process might not be as effective as it could be and machinery could break down. If machinery breaks down, production will stop. A lack of technology might also mean that a business cannot keep up with what their competitors are doing, eg if they are unable to use social media to sell products but their competitors are, then they might lose customers. Selling products via social media is known as social commerce or s-commerce.

Other internal factors that impact on the business include the culture within the organisation and also the decision-making process.

Corporate culture

This can be defined as *'the values, beliefs and norms related to the organisation that is shared by all its members'.*

Corporate culture is sometimes referred to as organisational culture. It consists of everything to do with the organisation including its values, emotions, beliefs and the language used. It is also to do with the attitude and behaviours that members of the organisation adopt because of the culture within the organisation. It is established from the beginning of the organisation's life and reflects the different activities (formal and informal), policies and procedures that the organisation has. The different management styles adopted by senior managers may also influence the culture of an organisation.

The benefits of having a strong corporate culture are:

- Employees feel they are part of, and belong to, the organisation; this can provide them with a sense of security and can improve motivation.

- It can motivate staff, which in turn will lead to improved efficiency and higher productivity.

- It can create positive relationships within the organisation that will enable better communication and decision-making.

- Employee loyalty can be increased, which will decrease staff turnover and staff absence rates.

- The image and identity of the organisation can be improved, which will be visible to all stakeholders.

- Customer loyalty might be higher because they associate themselves with the identity (eg logos, uniform and store design) of the organisation. It may also be recognisable across the globe if it is a multinational organisation.

- There will be consistency across the organisation which will allow employees to work in different locations or branches if necessary.

When trying to establish a positive corporate culture within an organisation, several factors need to be considered:

- The vision and aims of the organisation; these normally come from the original owners and/or shareholders.

- The opinions and views of employees; consulting employees on matters will help to encourage good working relationships and improve motivation.

- The design of stores, logos and uniforms. This is because these are visible and promote the identity of the organisation, though can be expensive to design and then to implement.

- How people (eg employees and other stakeholders) are made aware of the culture. This might involve holding events, which could be costly.

- The policies and procedures that the organisation has. These lay down the expectation and behaviour expected and will have an impact on corporate culture.

Decision-making

Managers and decision-making

Managers have the authority to make decisions on behalf of an organisation to enable it to meet its objectives. Decision-making involves choosing the best option from a range of options.

Managers carry out a number of activities and, according to Henry Fayol, a known management writer, have five functions:

Delegating and motivating could also be added to the list of functions that managers carry out. Managers have a very important role to perform in an organisation and have been selected based on the skills, qualities and experience that they have. Managers need to be able to work with a range of people as well as being able to make decisions.

Types of decisions

	Strategic	Tactical	Operational
What is it?	Long-term decisions concerned with the overall direction and focus of the organisation.	Medium-term decisions that are concerned with actions to achieve strategic decisions.	Short-term decisions that affect the day-to-day running of the organisation.
Who makes it?	Senior management	Senior and middle management	First line management eg team leaders, supervisors
Examples?	• To expand into a new country • To diversify the product range • To merge with another company • To introduce a new management information system • To change organisation structure	• To find cheaper suppliers to cut costs • To expand the range of goods offered - to grow • To develop a new marketing campaign to increase the number of customers	• What hours staff will work next week • To give someone a day off

Decision-making can take place centrally (ie in a centralised structure) or can be delegated to departments (ie in a decentralised structure). Make sure you go back and look at this section carefully on page 43.

Structured decision-making model

A structured decision-making model can be used to help managers when a decision is being made. The model consists of a number of stages that managers go through.

	Stage	Description
P	Identify the problem	Identifying the problem or issue that needs to be resolved by making a decision.
O	Identify the objectives	Establishing what needs to be achieved when making the decision.
G	Gather information	Gathering information from a variety of resources (primary and secondary) to aid decision-making.
A	Analyse the information gathered	Looking very carefully at and questioning the quality of the information that has been gathered. (Remember not all sources of information are of high quality. Look for sources that are reliable, accurate, timely, comprehensive and concise.)
D	Devise possible solutions	Creating a list of possible solutions to the problem or issue in question.
S	Select the best solution	Choosing the best solution from the range of solutions available. There might be internal factors (eg finance, employees and technology) and external factors that impact upon the solution chosen.
C	Communicate the decision	Letting different stakeholders know of the decision that has been made.
I	Implement the decision	Taking action to put into practice the solution that has been chosen.
E	Evaluate the effectiveness of the decision	Considering how successful the decision has been. (*This is explored in more detail on page 58*). Changes might need to be made once the decision has been evaluated.

> ⚠ **Watch point**
>
> The acronym POGADSCIE can be used to help remember the stages of the decision-making model.

There are advantages of using a structured decision-making model as well as disadvantages.

Advantages

- No quick decisions are made because time is taken to gather and then analyse the information gathered; the first option might not be the one that is the best and subsequently implemented.

- Time is given to think about and consider the range of options available; the strengths and weaknesses of each option can be considered.

- Factors (internal and external) that may impact upon the decision can be considered when time permits.

- The effectiveness and impact of each decision is considered during the evaluation stage and, where necessary, changes are made.

- Better ideas might be formulated when following a structured process that will result in a higher quality decision being made.

- The decision will be shared with relevant stakeholders therefore ensuring all those who need to be aware of it are informed.

Disadvantages

- It is a time-consuming process to gather information and the time could have been devoted to a different task.

- It might be difficult to obtain good quality information as it could be time-consuming and expensive.

- There might not be that many different solutions available to a problem.

- The impact of each solution cannot be seen until it is implemented.

- Instinct and gut reactions to a situation might be constrained because of the process that needs to be followed.

- It might be difficult to make a choice when a range of options are available and it may mean that the best option is not chosen.

SWOT analysis

An organisation might carry out a SWOT analysis (strengths, weaknesses, opportunities and threats) as part of the decision-making process. It can be used to identify the different internal and external factors that may impact upon the decision-making process.

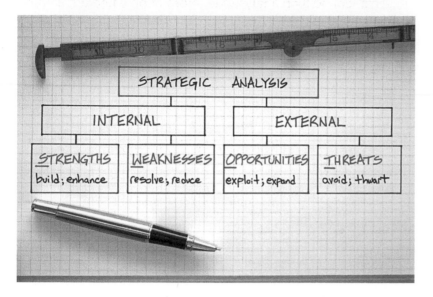

Strengths and weaknesses are about the organisation and its current position, whereas opportunities and threats are concerned with the external environment. An organisation will want to build on its strengths, improve its weaknesses, take advantage of opportunities and minimise the impact of threats.

Constraints on decision-making

A number of internal and external factors can impact on decision-making. External factors are explored on page 59.

Internal constraints might include the following:

- The availability of finance might mean that the most effective option cannot be chosen.

- The number of employees might limit what can or cannot be achieved.

- The skill and training requirements of employees.

- The ability and skill of managers to make decisions; more complex decisions will demand more skills from managers.

- The policies and procedures of the organisation might limit what decision can be made and, as a result, the decision might have to be modified to comply with them.

- The quality of information available; a lack of quality information might mean that a fully informed decision cannot be made.

- Employees might be resistant to change, which will make implementing the decision more difficult and time-consuming, especially if they disagree with the option chosen.

- Appropriate technology might not be available to implement the best decision and therefore money needs to be spent upgrading technology.

- Whether or not decision-making models (eg POGADSCIE and SWOT analysis) were used in the way that they are intended. Missing out a key step could make the process flawed.

ICT and decision-making

Information technology can play an important role when making decisions. Different pieces of hardware and software can aid managers and those making decisions.

ICT	How it can help
Spreadsheets	• Sales forecasts can be made to see what impact a decision might have. • 'What if' scenarios can be created to see what may happen when a decision is made. • Graphs can be created to make comparisons between different options. • Information can be handled more easily and quickly by, for example, using statistics to analyse information.
Databases	• Large amounts of information can be stored, edited, searched and presented using reports.
Word Processing	• Letters can be written communicating decisions. • Reports can be written exploring and detailing the decision to be made and the options available, and given to managers for consultation.
Presentation Software	• Presentations communicating the decision can be created. • Information can be displayed visually and communicated to a large number of people at a conference or meeting.
The Internet	• Information can be sourced from a number of places quickly (eg information on competitors could be accessed). • Decisions can be communicated via a website or via a social networking site.
Intranet	• Documents can be shared via an organisation's intranet. • Documents can be updated quickly and shared quickly but only to those within the organisation.
E-mail	• Communication can take place almost at any time or place (especially if using a smartphone or tablet computer with internet access).
Videoconferencing	• Meetings can take place over long distances between different branches and offices to discuss decisions.

Effectiveness of decision-making

Once a decision has been made, the quality of the decision needs to be evaluated. This means looking carefully at the decision made and thinking about whether it achieved what it set out to achieve and how well it achieved it.

Decisions can be evaluated by:

- Asking employees for their views (in other words, obtaining qualitative information) on how well the decision has worked and how effective they think it is.

- Looking at quantitative information (eg productivity rates and sales or profit figures) to see if the decision has impacted negatively or positively.

- Looking at employee absence rates (again, quantitative information) to see if there has been an increase or decrease in the number of days employees take off work.

- Measuring the level of employee motivation within the workplace to see whether or not the decision has reduced or increased this.

- Asking customers for their opinion by carrying out research (eg conducting a survey) as this will give first-hand information from their opinion.

> **⚠ Watch point**
>
> The method used to evaluate a decision will depend on what decision was made and on whom it impacts.

❓ Questions

1. Describe three internal influences on an organisation.
2. Define the term 'corporate culture'.
3. Suggest benefits of a strong corporate culture.
4. Describe three types of decision.
5. Give an example of each type of decision.
6. Describe the stages of a structured decision-making model.
7. Explain the benefits of using a structured decision-making model.
8. What are the components of a SWOT analysis.
9. Discuss the role of technology in decision-making.
10. Describe ways of evaluating a decision.

External factors

External factors are those outwith the organisation's control. Changes in the external environment impact on how the organisation functions both positively and negatively. The acronym PESTEC (political, economic, social, technological, environmental, competition) is a useful way of remembering the different types of external factors.

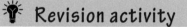
Political influences

Political influences come from the actions of government. We looked at the different levels of national and local government on pages 21–22.

The government at each level has different powers that can influence how a business behaves.

Political influence	Positive impact	Negative impact
A change in, or introduction of, a new law	• The new law may reduce restrictions on trade (eg opening hours of a bar) and allow the business to gain greater sales and hopefully profit.	• Policies and procedures in the business may have to be changed; this could be costly in terms of money and time as staff may need to be retrained.
Funding to upgrade infrastructure (eg a new motorway or airport)	• This may reduce travelling time between destinations allowing products to be transported more quickly, which will satisfy customers. • Access to locations that were previously restricted may enable greater trade to take place and therefore the business will gain more customers.	• There may be significant disruption during the construction phase that may impact upon the business being able to transport goods to customers on time. • A business seen to support the building of a new motorway or airport may not be viewed favourably by stakeholders if it aims to be socially responsible; this may damage the image and reputation of the business.
A change in the amount of tax to be paid	• If income tax was to be reduced, consumers would have more disposable income that they could spend on products, thereby increasing the sales revenue of a business. • An increase in taxes may benefit public sector organisations by providing them with extra funding they can invest in improving facilities for communities.	• If income tax was to be increased, consumers would have less disposable income that they could spend on products, thereby decreasing the sales revenue of a business. • An increase in tax for any business will reduce the amount of profit it earns and may reduce the dividend payment to shareholders.
New government targets to protect the environment (eg to increase recycling by 10%)	• The business will be seen as being socially responsible and can use this as part of the marketing campaign to enhance image.	• Steps may need to be taken by the business to comply with government targets, eg to reduce wastage, and may cost money to implement.

Economic influences

Economic influences refers to anything that encourages people to spend or not to spend money.

Economic influence	Positive impact	Negative impact
The number of people who are unemployed	• If unemployment is high, a business will have a larger number of people they can recruit from to fill any job vacancies. • If unemployment is low, people may have more disposable income they can spend on products, resulting in greater demand for a product.	• If unemployment is low, it may be more difficult to recruit people with the correct skills for a job vacancy. • If unemployment is high, people may be more cautious when spending money and this could result in less demand for a product.
Change in the interest rate	• It is cheaper to borrow money when the interest rate is low and this may enable a business to borrow money to grow.	• If the interest rate is high, it is more expensive to borrow money. If the business is experiencing a cash flow problem and relies on loans, this could mean that suppliers do not get paid.
Changes to economic policies by government	• Changes to economic policy may increase consumer buying power, thereby increasing demand for a business.	• Changes to economic policy might restrict the ability of banks to lend money and this may cause a cash flow problem.

GO! Group activity

Different economic policies exist. In groups, research one of the following economic policies and present your findings to your class:

• fiscal policy
• monetary policy
• supply-side policies

Try to find out the purpose of the policy and the different methods that the policy can employ to achieve different goals. Find examples of recent articles from the news that highlight the policy in action. Is the policy having a positive or negative impact? Why?

Skills

• Research
• Communication
• Thinking
• Decision-making

Make the link

Higher Economics explores economic policies in more depth.

Social influences

Social influences are those that are concerned with changing opinions, values and people's beliefs.

Social influence	Positive impact	Negative impact
Changes in fashion trends and tastes	• The business can take advantage of new opportunities by producing products that customers demand, thereby increasing sales.	• The business will need to invest money into carrying out market research to enable it to keep ahead of what people want; this will cost money and therefore reduce profits.
Changes in demographics (the number of people who live in a particular location)	• Customers who were previously unable to be accessed because of their location may now be easier to attract to the business, thereby increasing sales.	• It will be costly to set up new branches and offices in new locations, thereby reducing profit.
Increase in the number of family-friendly arrangements employers need to offer	• It is easier to recruit employees who have the appropriate skills but who want to work flexibly (eg part-time or job-share), thereby increasing the potential number of employees from which the business can choose.	• It may not suit the requirements of the business to have employees working flexibly and additional employees may need to be provided, which is costly.

Technological factors

Technology is changing very rapidly and has a huge impact on business. More and more people are using technology to communicate with each other and to do business.

Some recent technological developments include:

Tablet computers	These are keyboard-less computers that let the user do most of the tasks a standard computer or laptop would perform. The steady growth of applications (apps) that allow people to do business and communicate with each other shows their popularity on these devices (and also on mobile phones).
Wireless technology	This means using technology without wires while on the move. Many public transport operators provide wireless access to the internet for their passengers.
Web 2.0	This technology allows people to interact with each other, eg via social networking sites, blogs and wikis. It is popular with businesses for advertising their products and for communicating with customers.
Cloud computing	This is becoming popular in managing business information. Information is stored on the internet – in the cloud – and often means cheaper IT and staffing costs for a business.
S-commerce	Buying and selling through a social networking site, eg Facebook.
4G	Fourth generation (4G) mobile technology will provide people with superfast broadband speeds through their mobile phone. It is slowly being rolled out across the UK, but will enable a business to communicate much more quickly and to download information from the internet faster.

GO! Paired or group activity

Choose a recent development in technology (you can use one from the table above or choose your own). Prepare an information sheet that:

- Describes what your piece of technology is and its purpose
- Suggests different ways it could be used in a business
- Discusses the advantages and disadvantages of the piece of technology

E-mail a copy of your information sheet to the rest of your class so that they have a copy of it. Alternatively, you could post your information sheet into a blog for people to access.

Skills

- Research
- ICT
- Thinking
- Enterprise

Make the link

There are examples throughout these Course Notes of how technology can be used in business.

Technological influence	Positive impact	Negative impact
New piece of technology becomes available (eg tablet computer)	• This may allow tasks to be completed more quickly and therefore frees up time that can be spent on other tasks.	• Technology can be expensive to purchase and maintain; this would result in less profit. • Employees may require training in the use of technology, which can be expensive and time-consuming.
Growth of s-commerce (buying and selling through a social networking site)	• This will increase the number of customers that can be accessed, thereby increasing market share. • Updates can be made very quickly to social media sites, making communicating with customers instant.	• Procedures and processes will be required to manage orders received via s-commerce; this could be time-consuming to create and implement. • Employees may require training in the use of s-commerce which can be expensive and time-consuming.

Environmental influences

Businesses are becoming more aware of the need to be environmentally friendly and sustainable (in response to having to be more socially responsible) and are operating increasingly ethically.

> **Make the link**
>
> Environmental issues in relation to production are explored in Chapter 7.

Environmental influence	Positive impact	Negative impact
Changes in the weather	• Depending on the product being sold, a certain temperature may increase demand (eg demand for ice cream goes up when it is hot), thereby increasing sales.	• Depending on the product being sold, a certain temperature may reduce the quantity of a product that can be supplied (eg a very wet summer would reduce the quantity of strawberries available be sold), thereby reducing sales. • Bad weather might mean that orders cannot be delivered on time, resulting in unhappy customers.
Increased pressure to recycle	• The business will be seen as being socially responsible and can use this as part of the marketing campaign to enhance their image.	• It will cost money to provide recycling facilities, thereby reducing profit.

Competition influences

A competitor is a business that provides the same product as another business.

Competition influence	Positive impact	Negative impact
New competitor entering the market	• This might be good for consumers because competition can encourage businesses to provide loyalty schemes and reduce prices.	• A business may have to provide discounts to customers to retain their loyalty and this can be costly.
Competitor introducing a new product	• This will give customers a wide range of products to choose from. • It might give a business an idea that they can develop themselves even better to gain customers.	• It will cost money to carry out market research to try and stay ahead of what competitors are doing and it might not always be successful.

GO! Paired or group activity

Do some research and find an example of an external influence that has had an impact on a business recently. Present your findings to your class or ask your teacher to create a discussion forum to post your findings.

Make sure you:

- Clearly describe the external influence.
- Discuss the positive impact the external influence has had.
- Discuss the negative impact the external influence has had.

Skills

- Decision-making
- Communication
- Research
- ICT

Make the link

External influences can have a positive and negative impact on customers as well as on businesses.

? Questions

1. What are external factors?
2. Give two examples of each external factor.
3. Describe the impact of economic policy on a business.
4. Discuss the impact of environmental influences on a business.
5. Suggest reasons why businesses have to take account of external factors.
6. Describe each of the following technologies:
   - S-commerce
   - 4G
   - Web 2.0
   - Cloud computing
7. Suggest actions that a business will have to take in each of the following situations to remain competitive:
   - Increase in interest rates
   - Growth of s-commerce
   - Changes in fashion
   - Changes in demographics

Stakeholders

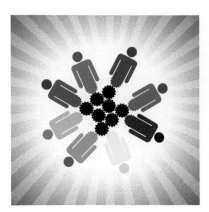

At National 5, we explored stakeholder interest and influence. At Higher level we need to think about the **interdependence** each stakeholder has and also the **conflict** that can exist between different stakeholders.

- **Interdependence** – why a stakeholder needs another stakeholder.

- **Conflict** – the disagreements that can occur between different stakeholders.

In the table below, owners could be shareholders and/or managers depending on the type of business being discussed.

Stakeholders	Interdependence	Conflict
Owners and employees	• Owners need employees to carry out different tasks **and** employees need owners to pay their wages. • Owners need employees to be as productive as they can **and** employees need owners to provide the necessary job training.	• Owners want to pay as low a wage as possible so that their profit is high **whereas** employees want high wages for their work. • Owners want employees to work as many hours as they can **whereas** employees want to work as few hours as possible.
Owners and customers	• Owners need customers to buy products from them to make profit **and** customers need owners to provide them with the product they want. • Owners need customers to become loyal to increase market share **and** customers want to be rewarded for loyalty (eg discounts).	• Owners want to make as much profit as possible by charging the highest price they can **whereas** customers want as low a price as possible. • Owners want to keep costs low by providing the cheapest possible service they can **whereas** customers want the best possible service (eg after-sales).
Employees and customers	• Employees need customers to buy from an organisation so that they get paid **and** customers need employees to provide them with good customer service.	• Employees want customers to spend as much as possible to increase their commission **whereas** customers want as much discount as possible.
Owners and suppliers	• Owners need suppliers to provide products on time **and** suppliers need owners to provide them with repeat orders. • Owners need suppliers to provide a quality product at a suitable price to make a profit **and** suppliers need owners to pay their invoices within an agreed time to prevent cash flow problems.	• Owners want supplies for as low a price as possible **whereas** suppliers want to maximise their profits. • Owners want to wait for as long as possible before paying their debts **whereas** suppliers want paid as quickly as possible.

Owners and banks	• Owners need banks to provide them with affordable loans **and** banks need owners who can make repayments on time.	• Owners want interest rates on loans to be as low as possible **whereas** banks want to make as much profit as possible by charging higher interest rates.
Owners and government	• Owners need the Government to have low tax rates **and** the Government needs owners to provide jobs. • Owners need the Government to provide grants **and** the Government needs owners to regenerate local communities and unused pieces of land.	• Owners want low tax rates to maximise profits **whereas** the Government wants taxes to invest into the country, eg for the NHS. • Owners want to dominate the market **whereas** the Government wants competition to encourage lower prices for customers.
Owners and the local community	• Owners need local communities to support their business **and** the local community needs owners to provide jobs to decrease unemployment.	• Owners want to keep costs low to maximise profit **whereas** local communities want businesses to invest in community projects.

GO! Group activity

You have 10 minutes to think of as many examples as possible of:

• Interdependence between stakeholders
• Conflict that might exist between stakeholders

Other stakeholders you might want to think about include pressure groups, trade unions and the media.

⚠ Watch point

You must give both stakeholders in your answer when talking about interdependence or conflict.

Skills

• Thinking
• Communication

Case study

Premier Inn

Premier Inn, a brand of Whitbread plc, has over 650 hotels offering accommodation for its customers at a reasonable price. It currently offers over 52,000 rooms in a variety of locations across the UK and aims to expand this to over 75,000 rooms by 2018 (a 45% growth).

Premier Inn has a commitment to the environment and takes steps through its 'Greener Together' initiative to reduce water and energy wastage. It encourages its customers to:

- Turn off the lights in their rooms when they leave
- Request an invoice by e-mail rather than paper
- Re-use their towels
- Turn the tap off when brushing their teeth

Not only does Premier Inn encourage its customers to behave responsibly towards the environment but it has taken action as well. It has:

- Installed energy efficient light bulbs in every hotel
- Sourced suppliers of sustainable paper
- Taken action to work with suppliers to reduce water waste
- Started to install water efficient showers in its rooms
- Provided training to its employees to encourage the Greener Together initiative

Premier Inn opened its first eco-friendly hotel in 2008 in Tamworth, England, and has unveiled the UK's greenest and most eco-friendly hotel in Sussex. This hotel will use cutting edge technology to achieve a 70% reduction in carbon and a 60% reduction in water compared to other hotels.

? Questions

1. Identify the two external influences being discussed in the case study.
2. From the case study, describe two examples of an interdependent stakeholder relationship.
3. From the case study, describe two possible examples of a conflict between stakeholders.
4. Identify one example from the case study of how Premier Inn may have a competitive edge over its competitors.
5. Suggest benefits to Premier Inn of having this competitive edge.
6. Describe the method of growth being used by Premier Inn.

★ Key questions

1. Describe the impact different internal factors will have on business activity.
2. Discuss the impact different external factors will have on business activity.
3. Outline conflicts of interest that could exist between stakeholders.

Summary

This chapter provided you with an overview of the internal and external factors that impact on how businesses operate. It also considered the interdependence of and conflict that might exist between different stakeholders.

The learning intentions for this chapter were:

- Internal factors
- External factors
- Stakeholders

By successfully answering the key questions, you will have proved that you have grasped the main topics covered in this chapter.

1 END OF UNIT MATERIAL

Unit Assessment

To pass the Unit Assessment, you have to achieve each Assessment Standard. For this Unit, the Learning Outcomes and Assessment Standards are:

Outcome 1: Analyse the features, objectives and internal structures of large business organisations.

- Comparing features of large business organisations from different sectors of the economy.

- Identifying the objectives of large business organisations and detailing the importance of these objectives.

- Describing the internal structures large business organisations may use and justifying why they would use these structures.

Outcome 2: Analyse the environment in which large organisations operate.

- Describing the impact of internal factors on the effectiveness of business activity.

- Discussing how external factors impact on the objectives of a large organisation.

- Outlining conflicts of interest that could exist between stakeholders.

Your teacher will make sure you know what you have to do to pass each Unit.

> ⚠ **Watch point**
>
> The Outcomes and Assessment Standards give you an indication of the things that will come up in your Unit Assessment.

Exam questions: Understanding Business

- Describe and justify two objectives for a public limited company. (4 marks)

Make sure you read the question carefully as every word is there for a reason. It is good practice to break the question down into parts before you start to answer it – this will make sure you answer it as best you can.

• **Describe and justify two objectives for a Public Limited Company. (4 marks)**

The command words – your instructions on how to answer the question.

You must give two objectives.

Only for a public limited company

Sample answer

A plc might have an objective to grow. This means to get bigger by, for example, opening more branches. **(1 description mark)** It would want to grow to gain more customers and to increase its market share. **(1 justification mark)**

It might also have the objective to be socially responsible. This means to behave responsibility towards the environment and not to do anything that might harm it. **(1 description mark)** It would want to be socially responsible to gain a good reputation and to improve the image of the business. **(1 justification mark)**

Examiner's commentary

The candidate has given descriptions of two different objectives suitable for a plc. They have then gone on to give at least one reason why each objective would be suitable for a plc. **(4/4)**

Further questions for you to try

• Describe different methods of activity grouping. (5 marks)

• Explain the impact a narrow span of control might have for a manager. (5 marks)

• Suggest benefits of being socially responsible. (3 marks)

• Describe methods of growth that might be used by a multinational. (6 marks)

• Compare a tall and a flat structure. (3 marks)

• Discuss the impact political factors might have on an organisation. (4 marks)

• Explain the costs and benefits of technology for an organisation. (6 marks)

Check your progress

	HELP NEEDED	GETTING THERE	CONFIDENT
Sectors of industry	◯	◯	◯
Wealth creation	◯	◯	◯
Public limited companies	◯	◯	◯
Franchises	◯	◯	◯
Multinationals	◯	◯	◯
National government organisations	◯	◯	◯
Third sector organisations	◯	◯	◯
Objectives (social responsibility, managerial objectives, satisficing)	◯	◯	◯
Methods of growth	◯	◯	◯
Grouping of activities	◯	◯	◯
Span of control	◯	◯	◯
Organisation structures	◯	◯	◯
Relationships within organisations	◯	◯	◯
Changing structure (delayering/downsizing)	◯	◯	◯
Internal factors	◯	◯	◯

	HELP NEEDED	GETTING THERE	CONFIDENT
External factors	⬭	⬭	⬭
Stakeholders – interdependence	⬭	⬭	⬭
Stakeholders – conflict of interest	⬭	⬭	⬭

What actions do you need to take to improve your knowledge?

$864.00
$474.00
■ Beryllium
■ Manganese
■ Aluminum
□ Chrome
■ Nickel

$500.00
116.00
$627.00

175.00
08.00
88.00
290.00

$590.00

194.00

$235.00

$771.00

100
80
60
40
20

TOTAL SALES BY REGION

■ 14%   ■ 8%

■ 5%   ■ 11%

■ 11%

■ 5%

■ 20%

■ 26%   ■ Media
                                    ■ IT ■ Electronics
                        ■ Textile
            ■ Medicine
■ Electric power
Oil ■ Gas ■ Electric power

TOTAL SALES BY REGION			
REGION SALES	€	1 236 345,0	Copper
	€	1 896 354,0	Steel
X	€	2 569 345,0	Gold
V	€	1 893 543,0	Silver
!	€	7 595 587,0	Platinum
!	€		

Unit 2

Management of People and Finance

4 Management of People

From National 5 you should already be able to:

- Describe stages of the recruitment process.
- Describe methods of training and outline their costs and benefits.
- Examine methods of motivating staff and outline their costs and benefits.
- Outline current employment legislation.

What you will learn about in this chapter:

- Workforce planning.
- Recruitment and selection.
- Training and development.
- Motivation and leadership.
- Employee relations.
- Employment legislation.

Workforce planning

Workforce or human resource planning enables an organisation to ensure that they have the correct employees in place at the right time to meet the needs of the organisation. Workforce planning involves analysing what needs to be done in an organisation and attempting to match suitably qualified and skilled staff to achieve the organisation's objectives.

It involves monitoring changes and trends in the labour market to establish changes in employment patterns. It is essential to be able to identify and estimate which employees will be required in the future and whether changes to existing staff levels, contracts and working practices need to be made. Workforce planning also involves considering the skills that will be required to carry out future job roles and then developing the appropriate training programmes to meet these requirements.

Recruitment

At National 5, the stages of the recruitment process were explored. At Higher, we need to look at internal and external recruitment.

Job vacancies can be advertised internally or externally, and therefore are available to internal candidates only or to internal and external candidates.

🔆 Revision activity

Download and complete revision sheet 3 from the Leckie & Leckie website. This looks at the different stages of the recruitment process.

Internal recruitment

Internal recruitment is when the job vacancy is only advertised within the organisation and therefore only people already working for the organisation can apply for it. The vacancy might be circulated via e-mail, advertised on an intranet site or an advert put on the notice board.

Advantages	Disadvantages
• Job vacancy can be filled quickly. • Employees are already known by the organisation and, if chosen, will have been so because they have demonstrated they have the ability to do the job. • Employees feel more valued and can become more motivated and productive if given the chance of promotion. • Money can be saved on advertising a job, recruiting, selecting and training, thereby increasing profitability. • Existing employees are already familiar with the policies, procedures and culture within the organisation and therefore do not need to be given guidance on this.	• The opportunity to gain new ideas from a new employee is lost and this could mean that new solutions to problems are not discovered. • An existing employee with the correct skills or ability for the job might not be available, therefore the position may remain unfilled. • There might not be that many existing employees that can apply for the position. • If a candidate is recruited internally, this will consequently create another vacancy within the organisation. • Conflict amongst existing employees competing for the job might exist.

External recruitment

External recruitment is when the job vacancy is advertised both within and outwith the organisation and anyone can apply.

The job vacancy might be advertised in a number of places:

• In the recruitment section of appropriate newspapers or magazines.

- On recruitment websites such as s1jobs.com.
- In a Jobcentre or via specialist recruitment agencies.
- On the website of the organisation.

Advantages	Disadvantages
• People with new ideas can be brought into the organisation and can help enhance the effectiveness of the organisation.	• Existing employees who apply but do not get the job may feel unvalued and therefore lose the motivation to work hard.
• External recruitment may attract large quantities of applicants so that the organisation has a range of people to choose from (however, this could be a disadvantage as it will be more time-consuming to look at large quantities of applications).	• It can be expensive to advertise a job externally, eg in a national newspaper, and is usually a more expensive form of recruitment compared to internal recruitment.
• Job vacancies can be filled quickly using the help of recruitment agencies.	• A more thorough selection process may be required, which can be expensive compared to internal recruitment.
• Conflict that may arise between competing employees within an organisation if only internal recruitment is used may be avoided.	• There is always a chance that the wrong person is chosen as they are unknown to the organisation, despite employing a number of selection methods.
• Specialist newspapers, magazines and agencies can be used to find appropriate staff, eg for specialist posts.	

? Questions

1. Discuss the purpose of workforce planning.
2. Suggest benefits of workforce planning.
3. Compare internal and external recruitment.
4. Explain two advantages and two disadvantages of internal recruitment.
5. Explain two advantages and two disadvantages of external recruitment.
6. Suggest places where a job could be advertised externally.
7. Suggest how technology could help in the recruitment process.
8. Describe each of the following stages of the recruitment process:
   - identify a job vacancy
   - conduct a job analysis
   - prepare a job specification
   - prepare a person specification.

Selection

At National 5, some methods of selection such as application forms, CVs and references were explored. At Higher, we need to look at some other selection methods in more detail.

Interviews

Interviews are a common selection method. They allow the organisation to meet applicants, ask them questions and find out whether or not they are suitable for the job vacancy. They also allow the applicant to ask questions to see whether or not the vacancy is for them. Sometimes applicants might be asked to do a short presentation in the interview, using presentation software.

One-to-one interviews

One interviewer interviews all of the short-listed applicants and then makes a decision on who to select. This type of interview is not uncommon, but has a distinct disadvantage in that the interviewer may not like a particular person for some reason (eg personality) and this could lead to the wrong person being given the job. However, it is cheaper than successive or panel interviews.

Successive interviews

Several interviewers interview each applicant separately. Unfortunately, it means that the applicant has a number of interviews to attend. However, it does have the advantage over one-to-one interviews in that it avoids interviewer bias.

Panel interviews

A panel interview involves one applicant being interviewed by several people at one time. Each person on the interview panel asks a number of questions and each member has a final say in who is selected. Each member of the interview panel will compare their notes on each candidate before making a final decision. Someone will be appointed to chair the interview panel and there would normally be a mixture of genders for equality purposes.

Testing

A variety of tests can be carried out to help in the selection process. Each test will assess a different aspect of the applicant's abilities or skills and can confirm what the applicant has written on their application form or CV. Tests can be expensive to carry out and are time-consuming. They need to be carried out carefully because, just like exams, people can perform worse than expected because of the pressure and stress imposed on them.

Psychometric/ psychological tests	In these tests, applicants are asked questions that assess their personality. The tests can be used to find out what type of person they are and whether they suit the requirements of the job. Unlike some other types of tests, there is no correct answer and applicants should give truthful answers so that an accurate picture of their personality can be built up. However, this does not always happen and applicants might select the answer that they think the organisation wants to hear. This type of test can establish whether or not someone would fit into a particular culture (eg a sales-driven environment) or one that is highly pressurised (eg air traffic control).
Aptitude tests	This test assesses the natural abilities of applicants on the skills required for a particular job they are applying for. Aptitude tests might assess literacy and numeracy skills. These skills might be important for jobs involving lots of reading and writing and/or working with numbers.
Intelligence tests	Also known as IQ tests, these assess the mental capability of the applicant. It might be that an applicant needs to be able to process lots of information that is being given quickly in a pressurised environment (eg emergency services) and this test would help to indicate whether or not they could do this.
Medical tests	A doctor or nurse examines each applicant for any medical issues or concerns that may impact upon their ability to perform the duties of the job. A questionnaire may also need to be completed. Some occupations (eg pilots) have strict medical conditions that need to be met.
Attainment tests	An attainment test allows an applicant to demonstrate that they have a specific skill, for example in ICT. A typing test, for example, might be given to a potential administrative assistant to see how many words they can type per minute.

🔘 Paired activity

Many websites offer you the opportunity to carry out different types of tests. Search the internet for different types of tests. Try doing some of them to see how you get on!

🌳 Skills

- ICT
- Thinking
- Decision-making
- Employability

In small groups, choose one of the following jobs:

- Market researcher
- Quality supervisor
- Administrative assistant
- Finance manager

Create a list of interview questions that might be asked at the interview for your chosen job. For each question, give reasons why that question is being asked and what answer you would expect to obtain from it.

Think about any tests that might be carried out to help you make a decision on who should get the job. Justify why each test has been chosen.

Make a list of any other selection methods that you would use for the job with reasons why they have been chosen.

Skills

- Communication
- Decision-making
- Thinking
- Employability
- Enterprise

Assessment centres

Assessment centres allow an organisation to see a large number of applicants undertaking a variety of tasks in different situations and realistic work-related scenarios. They quite often take place over a couple of days. Applicants may have to take part in team building activities, role play tasks and deliver presentations. Tests may also need to be undertaken. At all points during the assessment centre, the organisation will be watching the applicant carefully and making a note of their communication, leadership, team work and problem solving skills.

Assessment centres are expensive to carry out as they require significant preparation beforehand and the organisation needs to have the necessary facilities to conduct it. Several members of staff also need to be available to supervise and conduct the assessment centre. As several members of the organisation are involved, it reduces the possibility of interviewer bias.

❓ Questions

1. Define the following terms:
   - CV
   - application form
   - reference
2. Describe the purpose of a job interview.
3. Explain two advantages and two disadvantages of an interview.
4. Describe different types of interviews.
5. Justify the use of tests in the selection process.
6. Describe the purpose of four types of tests.
7. Describe the purpose of an assessment centre.
8. Discuss the benefits and costs of an assessment centre.

Training and development

At National 5, we looked at three types of training: induction, on-the-job and off-the-job. You should make sure you go back and revise these. At Higher, we need to explore different methods of staff development, training schemes and work-based qualifications.

Continuing professional development

Organisations need to provide their staff with opportunities to develop as individuals and as employees. Training allows people to carry out their jobs better and gives them the opportunity to learn new skills. Staff development is an important part of being able to provide a high quality product or service.

Most organisations accept that training should not be provided on a one-off basis, but instead opportunities for learning should be continually provided. Providing opportunities for development is important in being able to achieve the organisation's objectives in a changing business environment. The Scottish Government has a life-long learning agenda and has invested significant sums of money into providing opportunities for people of all ages to learn new skills and gain qualifications.

A record of all continuing professional development (CPD) that an employee undertakes is normally kept and quite often when an employee is requesting training, they need to demonstrate how this matches what the organisation is trying to achieve. Evaluation after CPD is also carried out so that it can be discussed at the annual appraisal interview between the employee and their line manager.

Virtual learning environment (VLE)

Many organisations now offer employees the opportunity to participate in CPD through virtual learning facilities. This is usually a specific password-protected website that people can log into to access training materials.

Advantages	Disadvantages
• Can be accessed at any time of the day in any location. • Large numbers of people can access it. • Can be updated easily with notes, tasks, videos and other materials. • Saves on printing costs and is more environmentally friendly than providing hard copies of training materials. • Interaction between users can take place through discussion forums and live chat facilities.	• People need to be self-disciplined to access the facility and carry out the activities. • People may prefer face-to-face contact rather than virtual learning; it might not suit their own learning style. • Might be expensive to employ a specialist to set up and maintain a virtual learning facility.

Make the link

People learn in different ways. It is important to recognise how best you learn so that you can obtain the best possible results from your education.

Glasgow Kelvin College

Training schemes and work-based qualifications

Many organisations offer their employees the opportunity to gain work-based qualifications. Sometimes these qualifications may be assessed in-house by a trained assessor or may involve someone from a local college or training provider visiting the organisation to carry out the assessment. In Scotland, work-based qualifications include Scottish Vocational Qualifications (SVQs) and are available at five levels.

Advantages	Disadvantages
• A recognised qualification can be gained. • Training often takes place on-the-job. • Assessment is carried out by a qualified assessor. • The organisation benefits from having skilled staff.	• Time-consuming to complete. • Some people might not want to complete a qualification. • Costs money to enter someone for a qualification.

In some industries (eg plumbing, joinery), people learn their trade by carrying out an apprenticeship. An apprenticeship is when someone learns on-the-job and may attend a local college for part of the work to gain a recognised qualification. Apprenticeships can take a number of years to complete.

GO! Individual activity

Visit the website of your local college to find out what work-based qualifications they have to offer.

Skills

• ICT
• Thinking

? Questions

1. Compare on-the-job and off-the-job training.
2. Describe the purpose of induction training.
3. Define the term 'CPD'.
4. Discuss the benefits and costs of CPD.
5. Define the term 'VLE'.
6. Explain the environmental benefits of a VLE.
7. Suggest other advantages and disadvantages of a VLE.
8. Describe the purpose of an SVQ.
9. Explain the advantages and disadvantages of having a work-based qualifications scheme.
10. Define the term apprenticeship'.

Motivation and leadership

At National 5, we explored different financial and non-financial incentives that can be used to motivate employees. We will look at some of these further at Higher and also at different theories of motivation and leadership that organisations could employ.

⚠ Watch point

Make sure you can suggest ways of motivating staff and be able to give reasons why those methods motivate staff.

💡 Revision activity

Download and complete revision sheet 5 from the Leckie & Leckie website. This looks at the methods of motivating staff and working practices.

Motivation Strategy	Justification
Providing fair pay for the work that employees do	Employees will work harder if they think they are being rewarded fairly for their work. If they don't think their work is being rewarded fairly, this will decrease their productivity.
Empowering employees with responsibility for carrying out a particular task or duty	Some people are motivated by being given extra responsibility as it gives them the opportunity to demonstrate what they are capable of doing. Some people are not motivated by carrying out routine, repetitive tasks.
Avoid the use of temporary contracts if possible	People who are on temporary contracts have no job security as they are only employed for a short period of time. Offering permanent (or open-ended) contracts gives people the knowledge that their position is secure.
Provide opportunities for continuing professional development	People will feel valued by the fact that they are being given the opportunity to learn and gain work-related qualifications. This will encourage them to work harder and will also allow them to carry out their job to a better standard.
Offer incentives (eg bonuses) for achieving targets	Incentives such as bonuses can be used to encourage people to work harder and achieve more. Salespeople are often paid commission or bonuses to encourage them to sell as much as they can. People working in a factory might be paid piece rate to encourage them to produce as many units as possible.
Having an open door policy	An open door policy will encourage employees to talk to their managers about different issues. This type of policy may allow issues to be resolved before they become out of control.
Empower employees	Empowerment gives employees the authority to make decisions without having to consult their manager. This can motivate people as they are seen to be trusted to make decisions by the organisation.

Motivation theories

Theories of motivation can be used to help understand what motivates people. They can be applied in an organisation to motivate employees. Different theorists have different ideas about what motivates people at work.

Maslow's hierarchy of needs

Maslow suggested that there are five levels of human needs that can be satisfied. Each level must be satisfied before someone can progress to the next level, starting at the bottom of the pyramid. If something is not satisfied at one level, they cannot progress to the next.

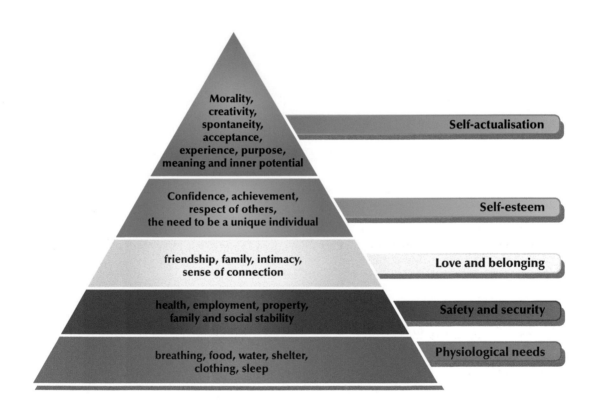

Adams' equity theory

Adams' equity theory proposes that what people put into their work (inputs) should be matched by appropriate rewards (outputs). When inputs and outputs are the same, people are generally satisfied. However, when inputs are greater than outputs, people become demotivated.

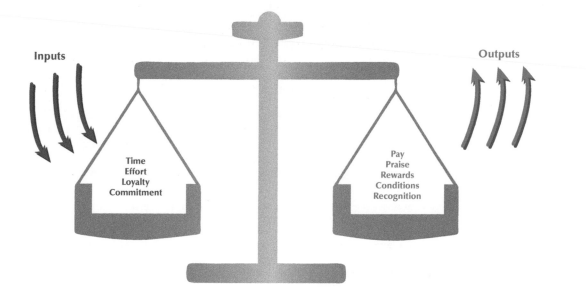

Leadership theories

Leaders in an organisation attempt to influence people to encourage them to work towards achieving organisational goals. A leader might be a manager, but might not.

McGregor X and Y

McGregor suggested that there were two different types of managers: Theory X and Theory Y. Each type of manager makes different assumptions about their employees and this influences how the leader behaves.

Theory X	Theory Y
The Theory X leader believes that employees do not like work and try to avoid it. It is assumed that employees have no drive or ambition and are not interested in being given responsibility or empowerment. As a result, the leader has to exercise tight control over what is going on and make all the decisions.	The Theory Y leader believes that work provides people with satisfaction and a sense of achievement. Employees are happy to work hard towards achieving the goals of the organisation. As a result, the leader provides opportunities for development and empowerment. The leader delegates responsibility to employees where they can.

Iowa leadership studies

Lewin, Lippit and White carried out a study at the University of Iowa. They believe that there are three types of leaders:

Autocratic	Authority and power rests with the leader. Decisions are made by the leader and are implemented using fear of punishment. Communication tends to be one directional and there is no opportunity for employee involvement, empowerment or delegation.
Democratic	The democratic or participate leader believes in consultation and communication with their employees. The leader believes that people are important and all have a valuable contribution to make towards decision-making. This type of leadership is often seen as motivating and can improve decision-making, as many people are involved in the process. However, it can mean that decision-making takes longer.
Laissez-faire	The laissez-faire leader does not exercise any control over their employees and people are really left to get on with things themselves. Support and guidance are only provided by the leader when requested. There is little direction given to the group, which can lead to limited achievement of organisational goals.

? Questions

1. Describe and justify three ways of motivating staff.
2. Describe the purpose of motivation theories.
3. Discuss the use of Maslow's hierarchy of needs.
4. Discuss the use of Adams' equity theory.
5. Compare a Theory X manager and a Theory Y manager.
6. Describe three different types of leaders according to Lewin, Lippit and White.
7. Suggest the benefits and costs of different types of leaders given in Q6.

Employee relations

Having motivated employees is a key factor to success in any organisation. Employees lie at the heart of the organisation and are crucial in helping it to achieve its aims. The relationship between employee and employer is important. Good employee relations can impact on an organisation in a number of ways:

- Staff turnover (the number of people leaving the organisation) will decrease which will reduce costs associated with recruitment, selection, training and development.

- The number of days staff are absent will reduce which means productivity will be higher and more customer needs can be satisfied.

- Employees will be more motivated and happier at work which will result in customers receiving a better standard of service that will encourage them to return and also to provide positive feedback about the organisation.

- Employees will be more willing to accept and adapt to any changes in the organisation as a result of the changing business environment; this will make implementing decisions easier as staff are not resistant to them.

> ⚠ **Watch point**
> Make sure you can explain how good employee relations can impact an organisation.

Good employee relations can be formed in a number of ways. Providing financial and non-financial incentives, such as those discussed when we looked at motivation, can be useful, but there are other ways to foster a good relationship.

Trade unions	Trade unions represent the views of employees on different employment-related matters. This might include pay, conditions, dismissal and any grievances. Employees have the option of joining a trade union when they begin a job but do not have to do so. There is usually an annual fee payable. Trade unions act on behalf of their members and have a much larger voice, more experience and are in a more powerful position to negotiate than individual employees on their own. (This is known as collective bargaining.)
Works councils	A works council is formed with representatives from across the organisation. It has the ability to access various types of information that relate to the organisation and it has the authority to take part in making decisions, alongside management, that relate to the workforce. Representatives from the works council might sit on various committees within the organisation.
Quality circles	See page 163 for more information on quality circles.

Contemporary working practices

We looked at the different working practices covered at National 5 in revision sheet 5 (see page 85). At Higher, we need to think about why there has been a change in working practices over the past several years.

- There has been an increase in employment opportunities in the tertiary and quaternary sectors at the same time as a decrease in the primary and secondary sectors (see pages 12–13).

- More people are becoming employed on part-time and temporary contracts compared to full-time or permanent ones to meet the needs of organisations that have to operate in a changing business and economic environment.

- More women are now in employment in both full-time and part-time jobs and there has also been an increase in the number of women who have management positions.

- Developments in technology have allowed more people to work out of the office either as homeworkers or teleworkers.

- The Government has encouraged people to become enterprising and as a result people are opting to become self-employed.

- There has been an increase in the number of small businesses opening up because of the increase in people starting their own business.

Industrial action

Employees who are unhappy with their working conditions or terms of employment, and where discussions have not reached an agreement, have the option of undertaking industrial action.

GO! Group activity

Make a list of different pieces of technology that could be used by people working outwith the office environment. Justify the use of each piece of technology.

Skills

- Thinking
- Enterprising

This would only be classed as 'official' when a trade union has agreed that this should take place. Different forms of industrial action were explored at National 5.

It is important to remember that industrial action does not always resolve the dispute between employee and employer. Sometimes the employer might threaten to make employees redundant if they refuse to accept the terms or conditions given to them.

💡 Revision activity

Download and complete revision sheet 6 from the Leckie & Leckie website. This looks at different forms of industrial action.

🔴 GO! Paired or group activity

Find an example in the news of industrial action that has taken place recently. Find out:

- What form of industrial action took place and why
- The consequences of the industrial action on different stakeholders
- What action was taken to resolve the dispute and how successful it was

Be prepared to present your findings to the rest of your class.

🌳 Skills

- Research
- Thinking
- Communication

Redundancy

Redundancy is when an employee or a number of employees are paid off because their job is no longer required or no longer

exists. It is not the same as 'firing' someone. It can happen when the organisation can no longer afford to pay the number of employees it has or when a demand for the organisation's product has decreased. By law, organisations have a strict procedure to follow when making staff redundant and must usually make redundancy payments to those people being laid off.

Employees who are not being made redundant may worry about the safety of their own jobs and the quality of their work can suffer. They may be required to undertake additional tasks or duties as a result of fewer people working for the organisation. This can consequently increase their own workload and may require them to be re-trained to carry out new tasks.

Grievances

A grievance is when an employee has a complaint to make to their employer regarding a work-related issue. They may be unhappy about something they have been asked to do or because of the way they feel they have been treated. Organisations will have in place a grievance procedure that will identify the steps an employee needs to follow when making a grievance. As a last resort, an employee can take their grievance to ACAS (Advisory, Conciliation and Arbitration Service) or to an industrial tribunal. ACAS is an organisation that specialises in resolving disputes and disagreements between employees and their employers.

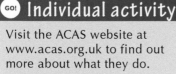

Individual activity

Visit the ACAS website at www.acas.org.uk to find out more about what they do.

Skills

- ICT
- Research

Appraisals

An appraisal is normally an annual formal meeting between an employee and employer to discuss the employee's work performance (their strengths and development needs). It is a two-way process as the employee will receive feedback from their employer, but the employee is also expected to think about and evaluate their own performance. An appraisal system aims to ensure employees are working to the best possible standard with the goal of achieving the organisation's aims. An appraisal can be motivating or demotivating for an employee depending on how it is carried out and whether or not it is seen as a positive or negative experience. At an appraisal, the following questions might be discussed:

- What is going well?

- What is not going so well?

- What could be done better?

- What action could be taken to make things better?

A written record of the appraisal meeting will be kept and where an employee has development needs, the employee would normally be given the opportunity to undertake CPD or training as appropriate.

Benefits	Costs
• Employees who have the potential for promotion can be identified. • Feedback is given to the employee by their line manager to improve their work; praise can be given for work done well. • Can be a motivating experience if the appraisal is positive. • Opportunities for CPD and training can be identified. • Targets for future performance can be discussed and agreed.	• Some employees might see the appraisal as a 'tick-box' exercise and not take it seriously or commit to it. • Can be a demotivating experience if the appraisal is negative. • It is a time-consuming process to carry out; other activities are not being completed when an appraisal meeting is taking place. • An employee might have too many development needs, which could result in additional stress for them and an increased workload.

Other appraisal systems include:

- **Peer-to-peer appraisal** – when a colleague at the same level of the hierarchy conducts the appraisal.

- **360 degree appraisal** – when the skills and performance of an employee are compared against others who work around them using a thorough self-evaluation process.

- **Informal appraisal** – no formal structure is followed; instead a chat between an employee and employer takes place; the employee might receive feedback on how to do something better or they might be praised for doing a job well.

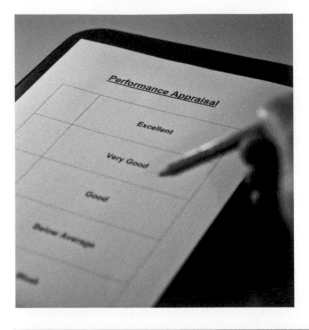

? Questions

1. Explain three benefits of having good employee relations.
2. Explain three consequences of having poor employee relations.
3. Define the term 'trade union'.
4. Define the term 'works council'.
5. Suggest reasons why a range of working practices are now offered by organisations.
6. Describe two advantages and two disadvantages of flexible working practices.
7. Describe each of the following working practices:
    *   hot-desking
    *   teleworking
    *   job share
    *   annualised hours
    *   flexi-time.
8. Describe five forms of industrial action.
9. Define the term 'redundancy'.
10. Define the term 'grievance'.
11. Outline the consequences of a grievance for an organisation.
12. Describe the purpose of ACAS.
13. Explain two advantages and two disadvantages of an appraisal system.
14. Describe two types of appraisal.

Employment legislation

The Equality Act 2010

The Equality Act brings together a number of different aspects of equality under one piece of legislation. Previously, different pieces of legislation existed.

The Act states that people must not be discriminated against on the basis of 'protected characteristics'. These protected characteristics are race, gender, sexual orientation, age, disability, religion, pregnancy and maternity. This applies not just to employees of a business, but also to the people who purchase goods and services. Managers of a business need to be aware of this legislation because they will need to take certain actions to ensure the business remains within the law. For example:

- When advertisements for jobs are being created, managers need to ensure they do not include words or statements about the person they are looking for that might be seen to break the law, eg they could not say 'a young person is required' as this would indicate age discrimination.

- Barriers to physically accessing the business will need to be considered and, where possible, action taken to make the business more accessible (eg by installing lifts or ramps to enable people with a disability to access the business).

- If an employee or customer feels that they are being discriminated against on the basis of one or more of the protected characteristics, the organisation has a duty to investigate this and take action where necessary.

- Policies may need to be created to ensure that all employees of the business are aware of the legislation and what they need to do to comply with it.

Non-compliance with the Act may result in prosecution.

> **⚠ Watch point**
>
> Be able to give examples of what an employer must do to comply with pieces of legislation. It is not enough at Higher to simply know what the legislation is – the impact of it is important.

Employment Rights Act 1996

This Act states the legal rights of employees in the workplace. It states that:

- Employees are entitled to receive a written statement of the terms and conditions of employment; this means that an employer will need to produce this and provide their employees with a copy of it.

- Employees have the right to an itemised pay slip; employers will need to have a record keeping system in place to record such pay information and to produce this for each employee when they are being paid.

- Employees have the right not to be unfairly dismissed; employers will need to have a policy in place covering dismissal from the workplace that clearly sets out the process to be followed if a disciplinary or dismissal issue became apparent.

- Employees are entitled to redundancy provisions if they were to be made redundant.

National Minimum Wage Act 1998

This Act sets out the lowest amount of pay a person can receive per hour. The current minimum wage (as of October 2014) is:

Age	Rate
21 and over	£6.50 per hour
18 to 20	£5.13 per hour
Under 18	£3.79 per hour
Apprentice	£2.73 per hour

Employers need to make sure they have the funds in place to be able to pay their employees the required minimum wage. This might mean having to budget carefully to ensure they can make the required payments on time.

Make the link

At National 5, we also looked at health and safety legislation.

★ Key questions

1. Describe methods that can be used to ensure there are sufficient human resources available in an organisation.
2. Describe and justify methods to motivate staff.
3. Explain the consequences of positive and negative employee relations on an organisation.
4. Describe the impact of employment legislation on an organisation.

Summary

This chapter provided you with an overview of the methods that can be employed to ensure that there is sufficient and suitably-qualified human resources available in an organisation. It also explored the importance and consequences of employee relations and the impact of employment legislation on an organisation.

The learning intentions for this chapter were:

*   Workforce planning

*   Recruitment and selection

*   Training and development

*   Motivation and leadership

*   Employee relations

*   Employment legislation

By successfully answering the key questions, you will have proved that you have grasped the main topics covered in this chapter.

5 Management of Finance

The role of finance

At National 5 we explored the role of finance and looked at some of the sources of finance for a small to medium sized business. At Higher, we also need to look at the sources of finance available to larger organisations such as plcs and multinationals.

The role of the finance department in a larger organisation is:

To control costs and expenses
Costs and expenses must be controlled to avoid financial problems and the need to borrow money to cover these costs. Where necessary, management might have to take action to reduce costs and the amount of money going out of the organisation.

To monitor cash flow going in and out of the business
Money coming into the organisation and going out of the organisation needs to be monitored. There needs to be enough 'cash' available to be able to pay suppliers, creditors and employee wages. Making profit and having a good cash flow are two different things.

To forecast what might happen in the future

Preparing budgets and looking at past financial records can help to identify trends and to see what might happen in the future. Action can be taken if necessary to avoid financial problems.

To monitor performance

Financial information can be used to compare one year against a previous year to see if performance has improved. This is useful to see if action taken in the past has worked and, where necessary, to take action in the future. Ratio analysis (see page 112) can be used to help monitor performance.

To provide information for decision-making

We already know that managers make lots of decisions. Financial information plays a crucial role in decision-making and will often influence which course of action is taken.

Financial information

Different pieces of financial information can be used by different stakeholders.

Stakeholder	Interest
Employees	• To check to see whether or not they are being paid fairly. (eg is the business making large profits but not agreeing to a pay increase?) • To understand why certain decisions are being made (eg redundancies).
Inland Revenue (HMRC)	• To check that the correct amount of taxation is being paid.
Shareholders	• To help make a decision on how to vote at the annual general meeting (AGM) of shareholders. • To decide whether to purchase additional shares. • To decide if the organisation is paying a fair dividend based on the profit being made.
Suppliers and other creditors	• To decide whether or not to allow more credit. • To show how able a business is to pay off its debts.
Lenders (eg a bank)	• To determine whether or not a loan should be given. • To show how able a business is to pay off its debts.

There is no doubt that decisions and planning are based on a range of financial information, but there are limitations to this. Not all decisions can be based purely on how profitable the organisation is. Remember, most financial information is based on past events and transactions. In other words, it has already happened.

When judging how successful a business is, financial information cannot be used on its own. This is because it does not reveal anything about:

- How motivated staff are.
- The impact of external factors.
- Future plans or product developments.
- How successful the organisation has been in increasing market share.
- The stage at which each product is in its life cycle.

Sources of finance

In addition to the sources of finance covered at National 5, the following sources are also available to large organisations.

Issuance of additional shares – limited companies could issue extra shares to new or existing shareholders. Plcs can sell their shares on the stock market.

Advantages	Disadvantages
• Large amounts of capital can be obtained. • Shareholders benefit from limited liability. • The finance raised does not have to be paid back in the way loans do.	• The selling price of shares varies daily on the stock market. • Share issue can be expensive. • Only a certain number of shares can be issued.

Leasing – businesses could rent equipment or premises rather than buying these outright.

Advantages	Disadvantages
• Saves on having to purchase expensive equipment outright (helps to improve cash flow). • Equipment can be changed regularly and kept up-to-date.	• Leasing over a long period of time might prove more expensive compared to buying outright. • The leased item is not owned by the organisation and is therefore not an asset to them.

Venture capitalists (or business angels) – provide large loans to organisations that a bank or other lender may feel are too risky. They usually part-own the organisation in return for taking the risk.

Advantages	Disadvantages
• Organisations who have a poor credit rating might be able to get finance from a venture capitalist instead of a bank which sees them as too risky. • Large amounts of finance can be obtained.	• Not suitable for small sums of money or for short-term purposes. • Can be expensive. • Part ownership of the organisation may be a requirement of the loan.

The stock market

The stock market is where sellers and buyers of shares in companies come together to sell and buy those shares. Public limited companies (see page 18) can sell their shares to raise finance. A person who buys shares in a company is known as a shareholder and is an owner of the company.

❓ Questions

1. Discuss the role of finance in an organisation.
2. Suggest the interests different stakeholders have in financial information.
3. Describe the factors not revealed in financial information.
4. Describe sources of finance available to larger organisations.
5. Explain the advantages and disadvantages of each source given in Q4.

Cash flow and budgeting

Cash is a crucial resource in any organisation. It is needed to pay bills, to purchase assets, to pay employees and to achieve different objectives. Most organisations have the aim of making a profit, but they also need cash on a day-to-day basis to operate. Making profit and having a healthy cash flow are two different things.

It is important that an organisation monitors its cash flow (or liquidity position) so that it can continue to meet its financial obligations and operate successfully. Failing to have a healthy cash flow can be caused by a number of factors:

- Having too much money tied up in stock.

- Too much time being given to customers to pay their debt (a long credit period).

- Not enough money being generated from sales.

- Too short a credit period being offered by creditors or suppliers.

- Too much drawings being taken out by the owners (or high dividends for a plc).

- Large sums of money being spent on capital items (eg machinery).

- Sudden increase in operating expenses.

Cash flow problems can be solved in a number of ways:

Method	Justification
Introduce a just-in-time (JIT) approach to stock management (see page 154).	This will save money being tied up in stock. By using a JIT system, stock is only purchased when it is needed for an order.
Offer discounts to customers as an incentive to pay on time.	This will encourage customers to pay their bills more quickly and the cash received can be used to fund other activities.
Increase advertising and promotion activities.	Advertising can raise awareness of the organisation and its products. Different promotion activities (eg special offers) could be used to entice customers to buy. More purchases mean increased sales and cash flow and reduced stock.
Sell fixed assets no longer required.	Selling assets that are no longer required will generate cash and, because they are not required by the organisation, this will not cause any disruption to the organisation's operations.

Make the link

Sources of finance (pages 100–101) can also be used to manage cash flow.

Cash budgets

To help manage cash and ensure control over future cash flow, a cash budget can be prepared. This is a forecast of the money expected to be received **(receipts)** and the money expected to be paid out **(payments)** over a period of time.

The benefits of preparing a cash budget include:

- It shows whether the business will have a surplus (more cash expected to come in than will go out) or deficit (more cash expected to go out than will come in).

- It shows whether additional finance is required to ensure the business continues to operate effectively.

- It helps control expenses by highlighting periods when expenses could be high.

- It helps to make decisions, eg whether to launch into a new product area.

- It measures performance of departments (see below).

A cash budget could be used as a target for the organisation and different departments within the organisation to work towards. In a large organisation, each department may have its own budget and the authority for controlling (and spending) this budget would be delegated to the department's manager. Management could compare the actual spending of the department with the amount budgeted, to assess the department manager's skills in budgeting. It would be the responsibility of the department manager to ensure his/her department stays within budget and, where necessary, take action to ensure it does so.

Case study

Fitness Fanatic Plc has prepared a cash budget for January–March. It wants to make sure it has enough money coming in to cover different expenses.

Cash budget for January–March

	£ January	£ February	£ March
Opening Balance	100	190	185
Receipts			
Sales	200	120	110
Total Receipts	200	120	110
Cash Available	300	310	295
Payments			
Purchases	50	60	70
Insurance	30	30	20
Wages	20	25	30
Rent & Rates	10	10	10
Total Payments	110	125	130
Closing Balance	190	185	165

- The cash available at the start of the period
- Money expected to come in
- Opening balance + receipts
- Money expected to go out
- Cash available less total payments

We can tell a lot from this cash budget:

Interpretation	Analysis
• Sales are decreasing	This is of concern. The company should find out why sales are expected to decrease (eg why is demand going down, is a competitor cheaper or are customers unhappy with the quality of the product?). Market research could find this out. The company might want to increase advertising and promotion to raise awareness of the company and its product.
• Purchases are increasing	This is of concern, especially since sales are forecasted to go down. Perhaps suppliers are intending on increasing their prices, in which case, a cheaper supplier should be found or a discount negotiated. Perhaps too much stock is being purchased. A JIT approach to stock management might be a possible solution depending on the product or service being offered.
• Wages are increasing	This is a concern, especially since sales are forecasted to go down. The company should find out why the wages bill is expected to increase. Perhaps overtime has been offered and this could be reduced. Payment methods could be considered.
• Total payments are increasing	This is because of the reasons above.
• The closing balance each month is decreasing	This is because receipts are decreasing and payments are increasing. A short-term source of finance might be required if this trend continues, to ensure the business can meet its financial obligations.

GO! Individual activity

Amira is the accountant for Stephens Plc and has prepared a cash budget for October–December. She has asked you to prepare a short report on her projected financial position by:

- Identifying areas of concern and/or strength.
- Analysing what might have caused those areas of concern and/or strength.
- Recommending what could be done to improve the financial situation of Stephens Plc with justifications.

⚠ Watch point

You need to be able to interpret a cash budget and provide solutions to cash flow problems.

	£ October	£ November	£ December
Opening Balance	2000	1200	−150
Receipts			
Sales	4800	4600	4400
Total receipts			
Cash available	6800	5800	4250
Payments			
Purchases	2000	2100	2200
Insurance	400	400	400
Wages	2500	2750	2750
Loan repayment	200	200	200
Advertising	500	500	500
Purchase of machine	0	0	6000
Total payments	5600	5950	12050
Closing Balance	1200	−150	−7800

Y Skills

- Thinking
- Decision-making
- Communication

? Questions

1. Describe the purpose of a cash budget.
2. Explain the benefits of preparing a cash budget.
3. Describe the consequences of poor cash flow.
4. Justify actions that could be taken to improve cash flow.

Final accounts

Organisations must prepare a set of final accounts every year. These are the:

- trading, profit and loss account
- balance sheet.

The final accounts provide a summary of the different financial transactions that have taken place over the last 12 months.

> ⚠ **Watch point**
>
> You should be able to describe the purpose and content of different final accounts.

Trading, profit and loss account

This shows a summary of the money that has came in and gone out of the organisation over the past financial year. The **Trading Account** shows the **Gross Profit** whereas the **Profit and Loss Account** shows the **Net Profit.**

Trading, Profit and Loss Account of Fitness Fanatic Plc for the year ending 31 December 2013		
	£000	**£000**
Sales		300
Lest Cost of Sales		
Opening Stock	40	
Add Purchases	150	
	190	
Less Closing Stock	20	
Cost of Goods Sold		170
GROSS PROFIT		130
Less Expenses:		
Rent	10	
Advertising	8	
Electricity	3	
Telephone	15	
Wages	10	46
NET PROFIT		84

The amount of money made from buying and selling (**Sales** less **Cost of Sales**)

Items that need to be paid for.

The profit made after expenses have been subtracted from the Gross Profit. (It could be a net loss)

Case study

A summary of the financial position of Fitness Fanatic Plc for the past three years is given below.

	2011 £000	2012 £000	2013 £000
Sales	300	280	260
Gross Profit	130	110	110
Expenses	46	52	55
Net Profit	84	58	55

Interpretation	Analysis
• Sales are decreasing	This is of concern. The company should find out why sales have decreased over the three-year period. (For example why is demand going down, is a competitor cheaper or are customers unhappy with the quality of the product?) Market research could find this out. The company might want to increase advertising and promotion to raise awareness of the company and its product.
• Gross profit has decreased then levelled off	Gross profit has decreased at the same time as sales have decreased; this is to be expected. However, in Year 3, gross profit has remained the same yet sales have decreased. This would indicate that the cost of sales (eg purchases) was too high in Year 2 in comparison to sales.
• Expenses are increasing	Expenses have increased yet sales have decreased at the same time. This is of concern. The company should investigate why expenses are increasing and take action where necessary (eg seek alternatives).
• Net profit is decreasing	This is of concern but is to be expected in light of the points above. The net profit took its steepest decrease from Year 1 to Year 2 and not so much in Year 3, which is positive. When the final accounts for Year 4 are published, they might reveal that the situation is more stable.

Balance sheet

The **Balance Sheet** shows the value (worth) of an organisation at a particular point in time. It shows what the organisation owns (assets) and what debts (liabilities) it has.

Items owned by the organisation that will last for longer than one year.

Items of short-term worth to the organisation, normally less than a year.

Liabilities are debts. Current liabilities are short-term debts. Long-term liabilities are long-term debts.

Current Assets less Current Liabilities. It shows how easily an organisation can pay its short-term debts.

Shows how the business has been financed (eg share capital - the value of shares sold).

Payment to shareholders for having shares.

People who owe the business money having bought goods on credit.

People who the organisation owes money to (eg a supplier).

The value of the business at the end of the financial year.

Balance Sheet of Fitness Fanatic Plc as at 31 December 2013		
	£000	£000
FIXED ASSETS		
Premises		250
Equipment		100
Vehicles		<u>50</u>
		400
CURRENT ASSETS		
Closing Stock	20	
Debtors	40	
Bank	<u>50</u>	
	110	
Less Current Liabilities		
Creditors	25	
Working Capital		85
Capital Employed		<u>**485**</u>
Financed By		
Share Capital		420
Add Net Profit		<u>84</u>
		504
Less Dividends		<u>19</u>
		<u>**485**</u>

Case study

A summary of the financial position of Fitness Fanatic Plc for the past 3 years is given below.

	2011 £000	2012 £000	2013 £000
Fixed Assets	380	380	400
Current Assets	125	130	110
Current Liabilities	45	40	25
Capital Employed	460	470	485
Financed by	475	480	504
Dividends	15	10	19

Interpretation	Analysis
• Value of fixed assets has increased	This is positive provided the business has adequate cash-flow to pay its short-term debts. The working capital figure (current assets less current liabilities) would confirm that this is satisfactory.
• Value of current assets has been variable	The value of current assets has not remained constant over the three-year period. It is lower in 2013 than in 2012, but 2012 is higher than 2011. The company should monitor this in 2014 to ensure that a decrease does not become the trend.
• Value of current liabilities has decreased	This is positive as the company's short-term debts have decreased over the three-year period. The company has enough working capital to pay its short-term debts.
• Worth of the business (capital employed) is increasing	This is positive as the company is worth more money.
• Dividend payments have not been consistent	The value of dividends has not been consistent over the three-year period. They are higher in 2013 compared to 2012 and this will have pleased shareholders.

Make the link

Specialist software packages (eg SAGE) can be used to record financial transactions and then to generate different accounts.

GO! Individual activity

Amira is the accountant for Stephens Plc and has provided you with a copy of the final accounts of this company for the past three years. She has asked you to prepare a short report:

- Identifying areas of concern and/or strength
- Analysing what might have caused areas of concern and/or strength
- Recommending what could be done to improve the financial situation of Stephens Plc, with justifications

Trading, Profit and Loss Account

	2011 £000	2012 £000	2013 £000
Sales	320	340	300
Gross Profit	120	130	120
Expenses	65	75	85
Net Profit	55	55	35

Balance Sheet

	2011 £000	2012 £000	2013 £000
Fixed Assets	580	580	550
Current Assets	235	220	200
Current Liabilities	155	145	135
Capital Employed	660	655	615
Financed by	695	695	665
Dividends	35	40	50

⑂ Skills

- Thinking
- Decision-making
- Communication

? Questions

1. Describe the purpose of a Trading, Profit and Loss Account.
2. Describe the purpose of a Balance Sheet.
3. Define the following terms:
    * gross profit
    * net profit
    * debtors
    * creditors
    * working capital
    * dividends
4. Give two examples of a current asset.
5. Give two examples of a current liability.
6. Give two examples of an expense.
7. How are plcs funded?
8. Give examples of when technology could be used by the finance department.

GO! Paired activity

Ask your Teacher/Lecturer for the name of a current accounting software package. Do some research into this package and find out:

* The purpose of the package
* The tasks that it can carry out
* The benefits of using the package
* The disadvantages of adopting this package

Be prepared to feed back to the rest of your class.

Skills

* Research
* Thinking

GO! Group activity

Look at different companies' websites and find their annual report and financial statements. These are real examples of final accounts for plcs.

Skills

* Research
* Thinking

⚠ Make the link

Specialist software packages can be used to record financial information and to generate reports.

Ratios

Accounting information can be analysed in more detail by carrying out **ratio analysis.** Ratio analysis can be used to compare an organisation's performance with its own past, that of similar organisations and also against the industry average. It can help to identify trends and/or irregularities over a period of time. When the results of ratio analysis give cause for concern, action can be taken to try and improve the ratio.

There are lots of different ratios that can be calculated, but in this course we will only look at a few of them.

Ratios can be grouped into different categories depending on whether they provide information on profitability, liquidity or efficiency.

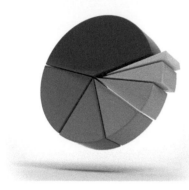

> ### ⚠ Watch point
> It is important to be able to describe the advantages of ratio analysis.

Category	What is it?	Ratios
Profitability	Measure of how profitable the organisation is. These ratios are used to analyse the organisation's expenses, cost of stock and the selling price.	• Gross Profit Percentage • Net Profit Percentage • Return on Capital Employed (ROCE)
Liquidity	Measure of how able the organisation is to pay its short-term debts. These ratios would indicate if an organisation needed to arrange additional finance to pay its bills.	• Current Ratio • Acid Test Ratio
Efficiency	Measure of how well the capital invested into the company is being utilised and if the organisation is performing as efficiently as it can.	• Stock Turnover Ratio

Profitability ratios

Gross profit percentage
This ratio shows the profit made from buying and selling stock.

$$\frac{\text{Gross Profit}}{\text{Sales}} \times 100 = \underline{\hspace{1cm}} \%$$

> ### ⚠ Watch point
> Make sure you can describe different types of ratios.

The higher the % the better. If in Year 1 the ratio was 30% and in Year 2 it was 35%, this would show that for every pound made from sales, more of it is Gross Profit in Year 2 than in Year 1.

Interpretation	Why would it change?
INCREASE in ratio from one year to the next	• Selling price has been raised. • Cost of sales has been lower because cheaper suppliers have been used. • Increase in marketing activities has caused demand to increase. • Better quality product being sold compared to a competitor and this has increased sales.
DECREASE in ratio from one year to the next	• Cost of sales has increased (cheaper suppliers should be located). • Stock might have been lost due to waste or theft. • Fewer marketing activities might have caused demand to decrease. • Fewer sales due to a better product being sold by a competitor.

Net profit percentage

This ratio shows the profit made once expenses have been deducted.

$$\frac{\text{Net Profit}}{\text{Sales}} \times 100 = \underline{\hspace{2cm}} \%$$

The higher the % the better. If in Year 1 the ratio was 25% and in Year 2 it was 30%, this would show that for every pound made from sales, more of it is Net Profit in Year 2 than in Year 1.

Interpretation	Why would it change?
INCREASE in ratio from one year to the next	• Gross Profit has been higher. • Expenses have been lower (possibly because cheaper alternatives have been sourced).
DECREASE in ratio from one year to the next	• Gross Profit has gone down. • Expenses have increased (the organisation should source cheaper alternatives).

Return on capital employed
This ratio shows the return on the capital investment made by the owner or shareholder in the organisation.

$$\frac{\text{Net Profit}}{\text{Capital Employed}} \times 100 = \underline{\hspace{2cm}}\%$$

The higher the % the better. If in Year 1 the ratio was 20% and in Year 2 it was 25%, this would show that in Year 2 a return of 25% has been made. For every £1 invested, a return of 25p has been gained. (NB not dividend).

Interpretation	Why would it change?
INCREASE in ratio from one year to the next (higher return)	• Sales have increased (due to reasons given for the Gross Profit Percentage ratio). • Expenses have been lower.
DECREASE in ratio from one year to the next (lower return)	• Sales have decreased (due to reasons given for the Gross Profit Percentage ratio). • Expenses have been higher.

Liquidity ratios

Current ratio (also known as the working capital ratio)
This ratio shows how able an organisation is to pay its short-term debts. It would indicate if additional finance is required to pay bills.

$$\frac{\text{Current Assets}}{\text{Current Liabilities}} : 1$$

An ideal ratio is 2:1. This means that it has double the amount of current assets compared to current liabilities. If the ratio was lower than 2:1 the organisation could struggle to pay its short-term debts. If the ratio is higher than 2:1 the organisation should consider how it would decrease this to ensure it is using its resources in the most effective way.

Interpretation	Why would it change?
INCREASE in ratio from one year to the next	• Current liabilities have decreased (eg fewer creditors). • Current assets have increased (eg more stock or more money in the bank).
DECREASE in ratio from one year to the next	• Current liabilities have increased (eg more creditors). • Current assets have decreased (eg less stock or less money in the bank).

Acid test ratio

This ratio shows how able an organisation is to pay its short-term debts without having to sell its stock. This is because stock can be difficult to turn into cash quickly.

$$\frac{\text{Current Assets}}{\text{Current Liabilities}} : 1$$

A ratio of 1:1 is considered acceptable. This is because it indicates the organisation can pay its short-term debts without having to rely on selling stock.

Interpretation	Why would it change?
INCREASE in ratio from one year to the next	• Current liabilities have decreased (eg fewer creditors). • Current assets have increased (eg more stock or more money in the bank).
DECREASE in ratio from one year to the next	• Current liabilities have increased (eg more creditors). • Current assets have decreased (eg less stock or less money in the bank).

Efficiency ratios

Stock turnover ratio

This ratio measures the length of time stock is held. If stock is held for a long time this could suggest that stock levels are too high. Alternatively, if stock is only held for a short period of time, it might be because a JIT approach is used or because the re-order stock level is low. The type of product being sold will also influence whether it is held for a long or short period of time.

> **Make the link**
> Stock management systems are covered on page 152–155.

$$\frac{\text{Cost of Sales}}{\text{Average Stock}^*} = \text{'times'}$$

*Average stock = Closing Stock + Opening Stock / 2

Interpretation	Why would it change?
INCREASE in ratio from one year to the next	• Increase in the cost of goods sold (eg purchases). • Decrease in average stock holding.
DECREASE in ratio from one year to the next	• Decrease in the cost of goods sold (eg purchases). • Increase in average stock holding.

Problems with ratios

There are some problems or limitations with carrying out ratio analysis. Organisations that carry out ratio analysis need to be aware that:

- The figures used to calculate the ratios are historic and do not show what could happen in the future.

- Comparisons between different organisations are difficult because the results are only useful when compared with an organisation of the same size and type.

- External factors (PESTEC – see page 59) are not taken into consideration.

- The results do not consider any workforce – related issues such as staff motivation or morale.

- New product development or launches are not considered.

Case study

A summary of the ratio analysis of Fitness Fanatic Plc for the past three years is given below.

	2011 £000	2012 £000	2013 £000
Gross Profit Percentage	58%	62%	65%
Net Profit Percentage	34%	32%	30%
ROCE	15%	12%	10%
Current Ratio	1.8:1	2.5:1	2:1
Acid Test Ratio	0.88:1	0.78:1	0.56:1
Stock Turnover Ratio	3.2 times	3.1 times	3 times

Interpretation	Analysis
• Gross profit ratio has increased over the three years	This could be because the selling price has been raised and has resulted in more gross profit. It could also be because cost of sales (purchases) has been lower due to finding a new supplier.
• Net profit ratio has decreased over the three years	This is because expenses have increased – not cost of sales otherwise the gross profit ratio would have decreased and it hasn't. The organisation should seek cheaper alternatives to lower its expenses, eg cheaper electricity provider.
• ROCE has decreased over the three years	This means shareholders are not receiving as much of a return on their investment. This is likely to be because expenses have increased as shown by the decrease in the net profit percentage ratio.
• Current ratio has been variable over the past three years	The ideal ratio is 2:1 and has been this or greater in all years except 2011. However, given the fact that the ratio in 2012 and 2013 is positive, this should be monitored to ensure that it remains around 2:1.
• Acid test ratio has decreased over the past three years	An ideal ratio is 1:1 and it has been below this in all three years and continues to decrease. This means the organisation does not have enough current assets to pay its short-term debts without having to resort to selling stock.
• Stock turnover ratio has decreased over the three years	There has been a decrease in the cost of goods sold, as confirmed by the increase in the gross profit percentage ratio.

GO! Individual activity

Amira is the accountant for Stephens Plc and has provided you with a copy of the ratios for the company for the past three years. She has asked you to prepare a short report:

- Identifying trends in the ratios given
- Analysing what might have caused ratios to increase or decrease
- Recommending what could be done to improve each ratio of Stephens Plc, with justifications

	2011 £000	2012 £000	2013 £000
Gross Profit Percentage	66%	63%	60%
Net Profit Percentage	28%	30%	32%
ROCE	22%	13%	16%
Current Ratio	2.4:1	2.2:1	1:9
Acid Test Ratio	0.7:1	0.6:1	0.5:1
Stock Turnover Ratio	4.8 times	4.4 times	4 times

Skills

- Thinking
- Decision-making
- Communication

★ Key questions

1. Describe and justify sources of finance that a large organisation could use.
2. Describe the purpose of a cash budget.
3. Describe features of two final accounting statements.
4. Describe one profitability, one liquidity and one efficiency ratio.
5. Describe the advantages and limitations of carrying out ratio analysis.

Summary

This chapter provided you with an overview of the finance function and the purpose and content of different financial statements. Sources of finance and ratio analysis were also explored.

The learning intentions for this chapter were:

- The role of finance

- Sources of finance

- Cash flow and budgeting

- Final accounts

- Ratios

By successfully answering the key questions, you will have proved that you have grasped the main topics covered in this chapter.

2 END OF UNIT MATERIAL

Unit Assessment

To pass the Unit Assessment, you have to achieve each Assessment Standard. For this Unit, the Learning Outcomes and Assessment Standards are:

Outcome 1: Apply knowledge and understanding of how the management of people can meet the objectives of large organisations by:

- Describing methods used to ensure there are effective human resources available.

- Explaining methods used to motivate staff to improve effectiveness.

- Explaining how employee relations can impact on the success of a large organisation.

- Describing the impact of current employment legislation.

Outcome 2: Analyse how the management of finance contributes to the effectiveness of large organisations by:

- Justifying sources of finance suitable for large organisations.

- Detailing the features of final accounting statements.

- Analysing accounting ratios and making business decisions based on the results.

> ⚠ **Watch point**
>
> The Outcomes and Assessment Standards give you an indication of the things that will come up in your Unit Assessment.

Your Teacher will make sure you know what you have to do to pass each Unit.

Exam questions: Management of People and Finance

- Justify sources of finance that could be used to expand a business. (6 marks)

Make sure you read the question carefully as every word is there for a reason. It is good practice to break the question down into parts before you start to answer it – this will make sure you answer it as best you can.

Justify sources of finance that could be used to expand a business. (6 marks)

> The command word – your instruction on how to answer the question.

> Plural – so more than one source needed.

> This is a long-term decision, so long-term sources are required.

Sample answer

Additional shares could be issued to existing or new shareholders because large amounts of capital can be obtained this way. **(1 mark)** It also does not have to be paid back (unlike loans that have interest). **(1 mark)** If the expansion abroad is not successful, this source gives shareholders limited liability. **(1 mark)** The company could also consider leasing equipment abroad to save them having to outlay large sums of cash for machinery and this will help to improve cash flow. **(1 mark)** It also means the company will be able to keep equipment up-to-date as they will not have to pay large sums of money to have the equipment replaced or upgraded. **(1 mark)** A bank loan could also be obtained from the bank. This is normally easy to arrange and can be done fairly quickly. **(1 mark)**

Examiner's commentary

The candidate has clearly justified three different sources of finance. As the question did not ask for a description of them, this is not necessary to gain the marks. More than one mark can be obtained for each source of finance. **(6/6)**

Further questions for you to try

- Compare internal and external recruitment. (4 marks)
- Describe and justify different types of interview. (6 marks)
- Discuss the use of tests in the selection process. (6 marks)
- Explain the benefits of using an assessment centre. (3 marks)
- Describe and justify methods that can be used to motivate staff. (6 marks)
- Describe methods of industrial action. (5 marks)
- Explain the consequences of poor employee relations. (4 marks)
- Describe actions that need to be taken to comply with the Equality Act. (3 marks)
- Explain the advantages and disadvantages of issuing share capital. (4 marks)
- Describe and justify sources of finance for short-term purposes. (6 marks)
- Define the following terms: (7 marks)
  - fixed assets
  - current assets
  - current liabilities
  - gross profit
  - net profit
  - debtors
  - creditors

- Explain methods of solving cash flow problems. (5 marks)
- Describe ratios that could be used to analyse the financial position of a company. (6 marks)

Check your progress

	HELP NEEDED	GETTING THERE	CONFIDENT
Workforce planning	◯	◯	◯
Internal recruitment	◯	◯	◯
External recruitment	◯	◯	◯
Interviews	◯	◯	◯
Assessment centres	◯	◯	◯
Testing	◯	◯	◯
Industrial action	◯	◯	◯
Employee relations	◯	◯	◯
Redundancy	◯	◯	◯
Grievances	◯	◯	◯
Employment legislation	◯	◯	◯
Technology in human resources	◯	◯	◯
Role of finance	◯	◯	◯
Sources of finance	◯	◯	◯

	HELP NEEDED	GETTING THERE	CONFIDENT
Cash budgets	⬭	⬭	⬭
Cash flow problems and solutions	⬭	⬭	⬭
Trading, profit and loss account	⬭	⬭	⬭
Balance sheet	⬭	⬭	⬭
Ratio analysis	⬭	⬭	⬭
Technology in finance	⬭	⬭	⬭

What actions do you need to take to improve your knowledge?

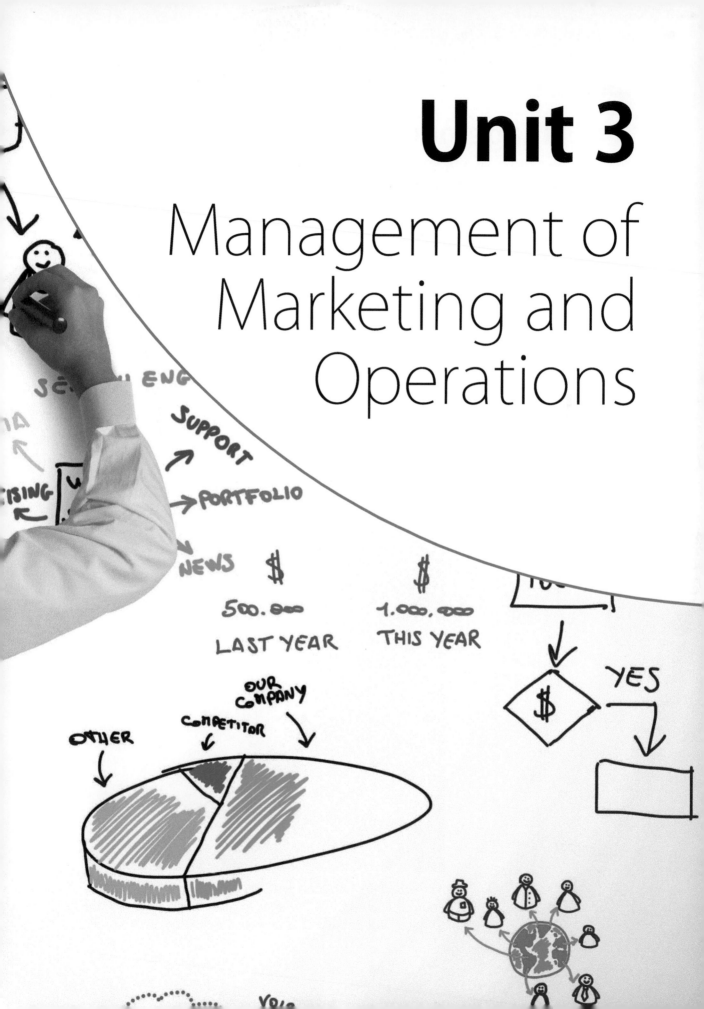

Unit 3

Management of Marketing and Operations

6 Management of Marketing

From National 5 you should already be able to:

- Describe methods of market research and outline their costs and benefits.
- Outline the stages of the product life cycle.
- Describe elements of the marketing mix.
- Outline ways ICT can be used to contribute to effective marketing.

What you will learn about in this chapter:

- Customers.
- Market research.
- Marketing mix (the seven Ps focusing on product, price, place and promotion)

Introduction

Marketing is more than just advertising or selling a product in a shop. It is about linking what to produce to what is consumed to make sure the needs and wants of the customer are met.

Most organisations will have a marketing department that carries out a range of activities. The purpose of the marketing department is to:

- Help achieve the organisation's objectives.
- Raise awareness of products.
- Increase the number of customers in a market (ie achieve market growth).
- Inform customers about products.
- Anticipate what customers want.

Marketing **identifies** what customers want, **anticipates** the requirements of the customer and then attempts to **satisfy** these.

Marketing is a strategic activity because it impacts upon the whole organisation and its vision.

Customers

Customers are very important to all businesses. In National 5, we explored different types of customers by looking at market segmentation. We also looked at the importance of good customer service.

Organisations may market their products towards a particular target market (**differentiated marketing**) or at more than one target market (**undifferentiated marketing**). Focusing marketing activities on particular market segments can have its benefits.

- Products can be specifically tailored to the requirements of the customer.
- Prices can be set to reflect the market segment.
- Promotions can be tailored towards the market segment.
- The most appropriate place to sell the product can be chosen.

Make the link

The aims of an organisation will be closely linked with its marketing activities.

Watch point

Different businesses will focus on different market segments.

Market-led and product-led

A business can be market-led or product-led in its approach to marketing. In other words, it might have a market orientation or product orientation.

Market-led (market orientated)	Product-led (product orientated)
• Product produced based on what the customer wants. • Customer wants and needs are identified through market research. • Changes in social factors (eg trends and fashion) can be identified and acted upon more easily. • The market may have significant competition.	• Product produced because the organisation thinks they are good at providing it. • Little or no market research carried out as the needs and wants of the customer are not of importance. • The market may have little or no competition.

Consumer behaviour

Businesses will be interested in the behaviour of consumers to help them make decisions about their product and how it is marketed. Studying consumer behaviour allows them to attempt to answer several questions.

Question	Comments
Why do they buy what they do?	Some products might be bought for status, eg designer clothing might be bought as a result of peer pressure or as a status symbol.
What motivates them to buy?	What factors trigger people to want to buy something? Is the purchase necessary or is another factor responsible for making someone want to buy?
What influences buying decisions?	What pressures or stimuli influence where, when and how people buy? Has advertising had an influence, or a point-of-sale display? Does the store layout have an impact? Does culture have an influence?
What customer buys the product?	Which market segment does the product appeal to?
Where do they choose to buy? Why?	Where do they choose to buy the product? Is it online or in a shop? Why? What factors have resulted in this choice, eg convenience?
What do they look for when buying?	What criteria have to be satisfied when buying something? What questions have been asked?

Consumer behaviour is about trying to answer the 'why', 'what', 'how' and 'where' questions. It is important to be able to answer these to develop a successful marketing strategy.

Consumers have different types of buying behaviour depending on what they are buying.

Impulse purchases	Buying something without thinking, often in the spur of the moment. It might be because something has influenced the customer to buy (eg a promotion).
Routine purchases	Buying something because it is habit, eg going to buy a loaf of bread. These types of purchases will happen without much thought.
Limited decision-making purchases	Buying something that requires some thought before a decision is made. For example, thinking about whether or not a piece of clothing is appropriate for a certain purpose.
Extensive decision-making purchases	Buying something that requires a high degree of thought before a decision is made. For example, buying a new car or a house. These types of purchases might not be made very often.

Electronic point of sale systems (EPOS) can gather information about consumer behaviour that the organisation can attempt to analyse and then understand. When people make purchases in a supermarket or shop, the EPOS system is collecting data about them and their buying habits. Promotions, offers and mail shots can then be designed specifically for them.

Make the link

Consumer behaviour is linked to psychology as it attempts to understand how people behave.

? Questions

1. Describe four methods of market segmentation.
2. Give three differences between product-led and market-led.
3. What is the difference between differentiated and undifferentiated marketing?
4. Suggest two reasons why businesses are interested in consumer behaviour.
5. Suggest four questions that a business might consider when studying consumer behaviour.
6. Describe different types of purchases.
7. Describe features of an EPOS system.

Market research

Market research aims to find out what customers want and what is happening in the marketplace. It involves looking at what already exists (secondary information) and finding out something new (primary information). Market research can find out:

- The types of customers who are making purchases and their buying habits.

- How successful marketing and advertising campaigns are, and whether or not they are cost effective.

- What changes might need to be made to existing products to improve them.

- What customers would like to see in the future.

- How customers have reacted to, for example different products, prices and promotions.

There are two types of market research: field and desk.

Field research

This involves carrying out research to gather new information. As this information is gathered first-hand for a specific purpose, it is called **primary information**.

Field research methods include:

- surveys/questionnaires

- interviews

- observations

- hall tests

- focus groups

> ⚠ **Watch point**
>
> You need to be able to explain how market research can enhance the effectiveness of a business.

Desk research

This involves looking at existing information (**secondary information**) from either within the organisation (**internal information**) or outwith the organisation (**external information**).

Desk research might involve looking at:

- websites
- newspaper articles and magazines
- government reports
- textbooks

Make the link

All research has to be carried out ethically. A business has to make sure that it respects people's views, privacy and right not to take part.

Sources of information

	Advantages	Disadvantages
Primary	• Source is known and is therefore more reliable than secondary information. • Information is gathered for a specific purpose and is therefore relevant.	• Time-consuming to collect, which might delay decision-making. • Expensive to collect which will reduce profitability.
Secondary	• Easier to obtain than primary information. • Usually cheaper to obtain than primary information.	• It was collected for another purpose so might not be as useful. • The information might be biased, which would lead to wrong decisions being made.
Internal	• Unique to the organisation and is therefore relevant. • The source is known and therefore more reliable.	• Information might not be up-to-date or complete, which means a wrong decision could be made. • Computer systems might be required to store internal information, which would be expensive.
External	• Easy to obtain, saving the organisation time. • More information can be accessed through, for example, the internet compared to internal information.	• Source might not be known and could be unreliable. • The information might not be up-to-date, meaning it might not be relevant anymore.

Field research methods

Questionnaire/survey

A survey (questionnaire) involves asking people their views and opinions through a series of questions. It could be done in person, over the telephone, through the post or, more commonly, online, as well as on the street. Sometimes people might be asked for their general views on something or they might be asked to rate a certain thing, eg how much they agree or disagree with something.

⚠ **Watch point**

You may carry out field research as part of your Course Assessment.

Questionnaires are relatively inexpensive to carry out compared to other methods of field research and large numbers of people are usually able to take part. However, people do not always like filling in surveys and they might not always give an honest answer.

Survey Method	Advantages	Disadvantages
Personal Interview This is a face-to-face interview. A number of questions will be asked by the interviewer.	• Clarification can be gained on questions not understood. • Body language and facial expression can be monitored. • Information is obtained instantly.	• Time-consuming and expensive to carry out. • Not many people may be able to be interviewed in this way compared to other survey methods. • Researcher requires training to be successful (eg questioning techniques).
Telephone Survey People are contacted by telephone and asked to answer questions.	• People spread across large geographical areas can be accessed. • Less expensive than a personal interview. • Clarification can be obtained. • Information is obtained instantly.	• People might not like taking part in a telephone survey. • Large and/or time-consuming surveys are unlikely to be suitable for this method.
Postal Survey A survey is sent through the post, is completed and then sent back.	• People spread across large geographical areas can be accessed. • Surveys can be completed at a time that people choose and is more convenient to them.	• Relies on people opening the letter containing the questionnaire in the first place, completing it and sending it back. • Information is not obtained instantly. • Clarification cannot be gained; the survey has to be designed carefully.
Online Survey A website is used to ask questions and people simply access the website to answer them.	• Online software can often be free of charge. • No postal or telephone costs. • People spread across large geographical areas and countries can be accessed. • Online software can often collect and analyse the results.	• Online software that is free might limit the number of questions that can be asked. • People require access to the internet. • Clarification cannot be gained; the survey has to be designed carefully.
Street Survey Asking people in the street to complete a survey.	• Specific individuals can be chosen (eg based on their age or gender). • Clarification can be gained.	• Expensive to carry out as individuals need to be employed to carry out the survey.

Observations

An observation involves watching something and then recording what happens. It might be that the observer is counting the number of times something happens or someone does something, or what someone's reaction is to a particular situation.

Advantages	Disadvantages
• Numerical information (quantitative information) is gathered, which is easier to analyse than people's views or opinions (qualitative information). • Often people are unaware that they are being observed so should act naturally.	• Those being observed cannot be asked for their opinion as to why they did or did not do something. • Observers need to be trained in carrying out observations.

Hall tests

A hall test involves a product being given to customers to try and then their opinions on it obtained. It allows for first hand information about the product to be obtained and is relatively inexpensive to carry out. However, people might not be honest about what they think about the product as they have tried it for free.

Focus groups

A focus group is a discussion between a selected number of people and a researcher. People will be asked for their views on certain topics and the idea is to generate a discussion around these topics. It allows the business to gain an understanding of people's feelings, but this information can be difficult to analyse.

Sampling

When field research is being carried out, it is impossible to ask everyone for their opinions on something. Because of this, people have to be selected to take part in a piece of research. Different sampling methods can be used to select people to take part in research.

- **Random sampling** – randomly selecting people from a list, eg a telephone directory. These individuals must then be questioned. It limits interviewer bias as they have not selected particular individuals to participate.

- **Quota sampling** – selecting people to question based on certain characteristics, eg age, gender or occupation. The interviewer simply selects those who meet the given characteristic, but this can lead to bias. It is less expensive to carry out than random sampling.

? Questions

1. What is market research?
2. Distinguish between desk and field research.
3. Give three examples of desk research.
4. Give three examples of field research.
5. Give three reasons why market research can enhance the effectiveness of a company.
6. Describe and justify three methods of field research.
7. Distinguish between primary and secondary information.
8. Distinguish between internal and external information.
9. Describe two sampling techniques.
10. Suggest two ways ICT could be used as part of the market research process.

Desk research methods

Desk research involves looking at different types of secondary (existing) information. Some of this information might be available electronically through, for example, the internet. There are different types of information that might be analysed:

- **Written** – information that is presented as text, eg reports, text messages, e-mails, written text on web pages.

- **Oral** – information that is spoken and heard by someone else, eg in a meeting or on the telephone or from a TV programme.

- **Pictorial** – information presented through photographs or pictures in reports, newspapers or websites.

- **Graphical** – information presented through a graph or chart.

- **Numerical** – information presented through numbers, eg sales figures on websites of companies.

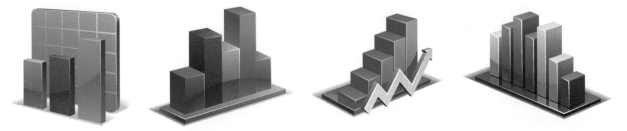

Information might be **quantitative**, in that it is factual and can be measured or counted, or it might be **qualitative**, in that it is based on the opinion of someone.

	Advantages	Disadvantages
Written	• Can be kept for future reference. • Facts can be passed on more accurately compared to oral information.	• May be unable to obtain clarification. • Requires a degree of literacy skills.
Oral	• Instant response is given. • Questions can be asked immediately. • Body language can be monitored.	• Points might be misinterpreted. • Requires careful listening skills.
Pictorial	• Information is presented attractively. • Significant points can be highlighted and/or emphasised.	• Complex information cannot be communicated. • Factual information cannot be communicated as easily as in written information.
Graphical	• Comparisons can be made easily. • Complex information can be presented clearly.	• Requires numeracy skills to create graphs. • The user needs to be able to interpret graphical information.
Numerical	• Financial information can be analysed. • Calculations can be carried out.	• Requires numeracy skills to handle and interpret numerical information.

GO! Paired or group activity

Different sources of information will have different advantages and disadvantages.
Choose three of the following sources and make a list of the advantages and disadvantages of each one:

- government reports
- tabloid newspaper article
- broadsheet newspaper article
- website of a competitor
- Business Management textbook

Be prepared to feed back to the rest of your class.

Skills

- Thinking
- Decision-making
- Communication

Make the link

Good literacy and numeracy skills are required to handle different types of desk research.

Marketing mix

The basic marketing mix consists of the **4 Ps** – product, price, place and promotion. Organisations must get the balance between different elements of the marketing mix correct in order to be successful.

At National 5, we explored what each element of the marketing mix is as well as why it is important. Before moving on, you should revise the following topics:

- branding
- product development
- factors to be considered before setting a price
- factors to be considered when choosing a business location
- distribution methods (road, rail, air, sea)
- advertising and promotion methods

Because organisations are now so closely focused on their customers, the extended marketing mix (or service marketing mix) is commonly being used and is made up of 7 Ps. The extended marketing mix consists of the basic marketing mix with an additional 3 Ps:

- **Process** – the different processes and systems used to deliver the service being provided.
- **People** – those involved in providing the service to customers, eg staff.
- **Physical evidence** – the location of where the service is being offered and what it looks like, eg store layout and design.

Process is important because customers expect the service they receive to be efficient and reliable. For example, when you place an order at a fast food 'drive thru' counter, you expect to receive the order within a very short period of time. The fast food establishment has to have a process in place to make this happen. New ways of providing a service have to be offered to customers through, for example, smartphones and tablet computers. Businesses have to keep monitoring their processes and updating them where necessary to make sure customers receive what they expect.

People is important because customers expect to receive a high quality service. Making sure the correct people are employed and then trained is important in achieving this. Rewarding them and encouraging them to work hard is also important.

Physical evidence is important because it helps a customer to distinguish one organisation from another. It includes the layout, design and facilities available within a store or where the service is being provided. In a supermarket, the fixtures and fittings within the store will create an impression as well as the signage and facilities available. A hotel user will judge the physical evidence of the quality of the bed provided as well as the facilities that the hotel has to offer, for example, swimming pool and restaurant. Customers are unlikely to purchase from a business if physical evidence is poor, eg you wouldn't buy meat from a counter in a supermarket that was dirty!

? Questions

1. Give a reason why businesses have to consider the extended marketing mix.
2. Describe the three additional elements of the extended marketing mix.
3. Give an example of each element of the extended marketing mix.
4. Suggest ways in which price, product, place and promotion could be changed to enhance the effectiveness of a business.

Product

Product is the actual (good or service) product being sold.

Product is important because customers won't buy something they don't want; market research identifies what customers want. The more products that are sold, the more chance the business will have of maximising sales.

An organisation can change the product by bringing out a new one or making an adaptation to an existing product. This will invite new people to try it and will help to maintain existing customer loyalty.

At National 5, we looked at the different activities that take place before a product is launched onto the market. We also looked at the basic product life cycle (introduction, growth, maturity and decline). At Higher, we need to build on this by looking at:

- The six-stage product life cycle.
- Profitability at each stage of the product life cycle.
- Ways of extending the product life cycle.
- Product portfolio.

⚠ Watch point

If you have time in an exam, a correctly drawn and labelled product life cycle can sometimes gain you marks.

Product life cycle

The product life cycle has six stages: development, introduction, growth, maturity, saturation and decline.

Stage	Description	Profitability
Development	Research and development of the product. A number of activities are carried out (eg market research, test marketing, a prototype is built). *Please revise product development from National 5.*	No sales, high costs. No profit.
Introduction	Product is launched onto the market. Product is heavily advertised and sales will begin to increase.	Sales are low and costs are high. Very little, if no, profit.
Growth	The product has gained greater awareness and sales grow rapidly.	Sales grow rapidly and profit begins to increase.
Maturity	Sales are at a peak and the product is well known in the marketplace. Extension strategies might be used at this stage to keep sales at a peak.	High profits.
Saturation	The end of maturity; everyone has the product and is no longer demanding it. This might be a single point of time or it might be for longer.	High profits before they decrease.
Decline	Sales decline as newer and better products are introduced to the market. The product is no longer wanted. Product is eventually withdrawn.	Profits fall and a loss might be incurred eventually.

🔵 Group activity

Find examples of products that are at different stages of the product life cycle. Make a list of different extension strategies that have been used to inject new life into some of these products. Think about how successful, or not, these extension strategies have been and why.

Be prepared to present your findings to the rest of your class.

🌳 Skills

- Thinking
- Decision-making
- Research
- Communication

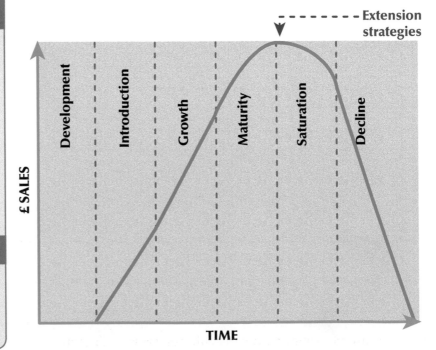

Extension strategies

An organisation wants to keep its product at the maturity stage for as long as possible. This is because the product is most profitable at this stage. To do this, they have to inject new life into the product to keep it selling. They do this by introducing **extension strategies** to the product.

- Changing the appearance of the packaging to give the product a new image.

- Changing the size, variety or shape of the product, as this makes it different from the original.

- Improving the quality of the finished product by, for example, using higher quality raw materials.

- Changing the method of promotion used to promote the product, for example, by offering a discount.

- Changing the method of advertising the product to reach a larger number of people.

- Changing the price of the product (up or down), to reach a different market segment.

- Changing the place the product is sold, for example, offering it online as well as in a shop.

- Changing the name of the product.

- Changing the use of the product so that it can be used for different purpose.

> **GO! Individual activity**
>
> Draw and label a product life cycle diagram.
>
> **Skills**
>
> - Thinking

Product portfolio

Many organisations sell more than one product for a number of reasons:

- To reduce risk of failure of one product, as one product might be doing better than another.

- To appeal to a variety of market segments, as different products will appeal to different types of customers.

- To increase sales and profits from selling different products, as customers will be able to buy a variety of products from the same business.

- To make introducing a new product easier, as customers will already be aware of the business.

- To increase awareness of the business, its reputation and its brand by having more than one product.

- To cope with products that are only demanded in certain seasons, as other products will gain sales at different times of the year.

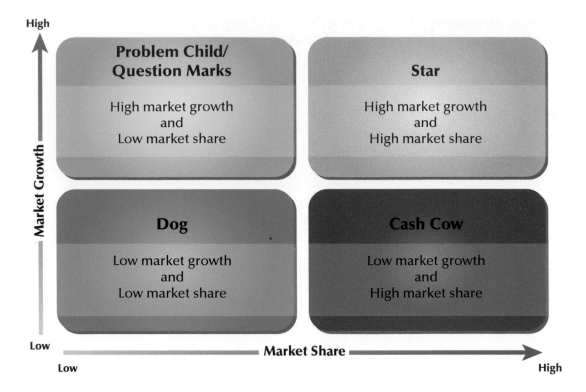

A Boston Matrix (or Boston Box) is often used to plot the range of products that an organisation offers. It can help the organisation to identify where products might need to be introduced or changed.

An organisation will try to have as many 'star' products as possible and will focus its marketing activities to try and achieve this.

There are some disadvantages of having a varied product portfolio:

- Costs of promoting and advertising lots of different products could be high and could result in less profit.

- If one product receives a bad reputation or image this might impact on all the products being sold by the business.

- Maintaining a varied product portfolio will involve a high cost of research and development.

- Cost of purchasing and maintaining machinery for different types of products might be high.

- Staff may require training on the features of different products which could be time-consuming and expensive.

⚠ **Watch point**

You need to be able to describe the advantages and disadvantages of having a varied product portfolio.

❓ Questions

1. Define the term 'product'.
2. Describe the six stages of the product life cycle.
3. Describe profitability at each stage of the product life cycle.
4. What are extension strategies?
5. Describe ways a business can extend the life of a product.
6. Define what is meant by the term 'product portfolio'.
7. Suggest two benefits and two costs of a varied product portfolio.
8. Describe the contents of the Boston matrix.

Price

Price is how much is charged for the actual product. It is important because customers will not buy a product if it costs too much. The price must not be too high compared to a competitor and it must reflect the quality of the product. The price charged should enable the business to cover its costs and also to make a profit.

The different factors to be considered before setting a price were covered at National 5. At Higher, we need to look at different pricing strategies.

Pricing strategy	Description	Justification
Low price	The price charged is lower than the price charged by competitors.	The product will be bought by customers because it is cheaper than competitors.
High price	The price charged is higher than the price charged by competitors.	The product will be bought by customers because they think it is of a higher quality than competitors.
Promotional pricing	The price charged is lower than normal for a short period.	The product will be bought by customers because it is on special offer and they are getting a 'deal'.
Cost-plus pricing	The cost of making the product is calculated before a percentage is added on for profit.	This strategy ensures that the cost of making the product is covered and that a profit is also made.
Psychological pricing	The price charged makes the customer think that the product is cheaper than it actually is, eg charging 99p rather than £1.00	This method tricks people into thinking the product is cheaper than it actually is and attracts them to buy it. It attracts consumers who buy on impulse.

Market skimming	A high price is charged for a new and often unique product. Often little or no competition. The price might be decreased once competition arrives.	A high price can be charged because little or no competition exists. A large profit can be made.
Premium pricing	High prices are charged.	The high price gives the product a unique and exclusive image. High profits can be made.
Destroyer pricing	The price is deliberately set low.	This forces competitors out of the market so that the business can then charge higher prices at a later date.
Loss leaders	The price charged is lower than the cost of making the product.	Attracts customers to buy. This then encourages customers to buy other products that are priced normally. Profit is made on the total amount of purchases the customer makes.
Penetration pricing	The product is introduced to the market at a low price and will be increased once the product becomes known.	Encourages customers to buy the product. Once customers are attracted, the price can then be increased.
Competitive pricing	Pricing the product similar to competition.	Attracts customers and allows businesses to compete.

Which price?

Businesses need to think carefully about which price to charge. Certain pricing strategies are only for the short term whereas some are for the long term.

Market skimming and premium pricing, for example, can be used as strategies for unique and exclusive products. This is because these strategies demand a higher price and consumers associate this with high quality. In competitive markets, competitive pricing or destroyer pricing could be used in the hope that it will remove competition in the market, allowing an organisation to increase its market share and also the price of the product in the long term.

Some organisations can charge high prices because other factors will contribute to their success, for example, their product being unique, little competition, brand loyalty or limited supply.

A business has to constantly review the price it charges because it operates in an environment that does not stand still. Changes in demand because of external factors are common, as is pressure from customers to lower prices. Competitors are also doing their market research and trying to introduce products that will be better and cheaper than their rivals.

⚠ Watch point

As well as being able to describe different strategies, make sure you can justify why they would be used.

Make the link

External factors impact on everything a business does.

⚠ Watch point

Make sure you can describe and justify pricing strategies that would be used for new and/or exclusive products.

GO! Individual activity

You have been asked to give advice to someone who is setting up their own business. They are confused by the different pricing strategies available and when they might be used.

Create a factsheet or leaflet describing different types of pricing strategies that are available to organisations and when they might be used. Use desktop publishing or word processing software to create your factsheet/leaflet.

Skills

- ICT
- Enterprise
- Thinking

? Questions

1. What is price?
2. Compare low and high price.
3. Justify the use of the following pricing strategies:
   - destroyer
   - skimming
   - psychological
   - competitive
   - cost-plus
4. Suggest and justify a pricing strategy that might be used for a new product.
5. Suggest and justify a pricing strategy that might be used for a product with an exclusive image.
6. Describe factors needing to be taken into account when deciding on which pricing strategy to use.
7. Suggest reasons why a business has to constantly review its prices.

Place

Place is about getting the product to the customer and where it is sold. Changes to where the product can be bought and how it gets to the customer may attract new customers.

Channels of distribution

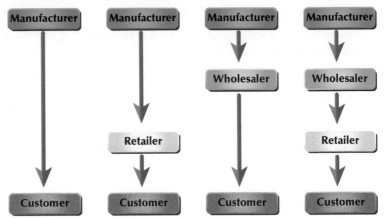

Make the link

The method of physical distribution (eg road, rail, air and sea) was covered at National 5.

Revision activity

Download and complete revision sheet 9 from the Leckie & Leckie website. This looks at methods of physical distribution.

Channel of distribution is the route a product will follow to get from the manufacturer to the customer. The route always starts with the manufacturer and ends with the customer. The four channels of distribution are shown above.

There are a number of factors that will determine which channel of distribution is used. These factors include:

- The actual product and its life cycle (products with a shorter life cycle may need to be sold directly to the customer to preserve them, eg fresh fruit or flowers).

- The image and exclusivity the manufacturer wants the product to have.

- The availability of finance.

- The reputation and reliability of wholesalers and retailers.

- Legal restrictions.

- The logistic facilities available to the manufacturer (their ability to transport and store the product from one place to the next).

Wholesalers

A wholesaler buys large quantities of items from the manufacturer and then sells them on to retailers, or directly to the customer, in smaller quantities. Many larger retailers do not use a wholesaler as part of their distribution channel because they have their own warehouses and transport systems (this is sometimes referred to as 'logistics', see page 156).

The use of a wholesaler has costs and benefits.

Benefits	Costs
• Distribution and storage costs are reduced because products might be bought in bulk. • The wholesaler may promote the manufactured product resulting in less cost for the manufacturer. • The risk of not selling the product to a retailer or to the customer is taken on by the wholesaler and therefore risk for the manufacturer is reduced. • Packaging, labelling and marketing might be carried out by the wholesaler. • The manufacturer does not have to worry about having to sell excess stock if there are changes in the business environment (eg fashion). • The wholesaler may provide information on the product for the retailer. • Retailers do not have to pay for expensive storage facilities to hold stock as they can buy smaller quantities compared to sourcing directly from the manufacturer.	• The manufacturer loses control over what happens to the product after they have sold it and may not like the way the product is being portrayed by wholesalers or retailers. • There is less profit for the manufacturer as they have not sold directly to the customer. • Loyalty and any associated benefits of this (eg discounts with the manufacturer) cannot be gained.

Retailers

A retailer is an organisation that distributes products to the customer on behalf of the manufacturer. Retailers stock a range of products from a number of manufacturers and wholesalers. The retailer will decide on the price to be charged to the customer and how to display the product to be sold. The manufacturer will decide which retailer to use based on where the customers are and what extra services (eg credit and delivery terms) they offer the customer.

Make the link

The changing business environment influences the popularity and growth of different retailers. There has been a change in retailing trends over the past several years.

Retailers benefit from sourcing products directly from a manufacturer because they can tell them what quantity they want and at what cost; larger retailers (eg supermarkets) may be particularly powerful at being able to specify what they want. Sometimes retailers can take advantage of economies of scale (the benefits of buying in bulk). Sometimes manufacturers will decide not to use a retailer as part of the channel of distribution because the product will face competition in store from other manufacturers' products and because it adds on an extra financial cost to the distribution channel.

Types of retailers

Supermarkets	Often very large organisations that buy large quantities and then sell them in their stores. They mainly supply food and drink but have increasingly started to supply other products such as electrical and home ware. Local supermarkets (eg Tesco Express) are growing in popularity. Large supermarkets have put many smaller businesses (eg corner shops) out of business in some towns.
Discount Retailer	They tend to provide non-branded products at a cheap price. These types of stores have become very popular in the UK because of the economic climate. The growth of them has resulted in other retailers having to discount their own products in order to remain competitive.
E-tailer	Shopping online and having the product delivered to you (eg through Amazon). This type of retailer often has lower overhead costs because they do not have to worry about having stores from which to sell their products. However, they often require large warehouses to store their products. They may rely on different logistic companies to distribute their products.
Convenience Retailer	Often referred to as the corner shop. This type of retailer normally has a small shop where a limited amount of products can be bought. They are often found in busy residential areas and are normally more expensive than supermarkets. This is because they do not have the same buying power as supermarkets and because they are offering a product in a convenient place for their customer.

Direct selling

Internet selling (or e-tailing) involves selling products to the customer through an internet website. S-commerce, using social media, is also becoming popular. An internet website is a collection of information in one place which can be seen by typing in a website address (a URL) into a browser such as Internet Explorer or Safari. An organisation may have a website to sell its products and also to advertise them.

Advantages	Disadvantages
• Customers worldwide can purchase goods. • Customers can buy online 24/7 from their own home. • Online discounts may be available as a shop is not required. • Product information can be updated and accessed quickly. • Products can be compared with others. • Convenient if access to a retailer is not available. • Stock availability can often be checked instantly and products reserved. • A website can be set up fairly cheaply.	• The customer is unable to see or handle the goods before purchasing. • Customers might not want to provide their credit or debit card details to a website. • Internet or computer problems might occur when ordering. • There is a time delay between ordering and actually receiving the good. • Items can get lost or damaged during transportation. • There is no personal contact with the organisation. • Relies on customers being able to use a computer and navigate around a website. • A web designer may be required to create a high quality website and this might be expensive.

Personal selling involves a trained sales member of the organisation selling the product directly to the customer. You commonly see it in shopping centres as you walk through. It allows the sales member to demonstrate how the product works to the customer and to answer any questions that they may have. Customers might feel pressured into buying the product and this might put them off. It also requires training to be given to ensure the sales member is knowledgeable about the product and how it works.

Direct mail involves posting letters or leaflets directly to the homes of potential customers. This allows for specific market segments to be targeted, covering large geographical areas. However, customers might not like receiving lots of mail in this way and might just bin it (we all know how frustrating 'junk mail' can be).

Mail order, buying through a catalogue, is another method of direct selling. It is convenient to the customer as they can look

GO! **Paired activity**

Think about your local high street or town. Create a list of the different types of retailers that exist. Use Google Maps to help you.

Skills

• Thinking
• ICT

through the catalogue in their own time and order when they feel ready. It also reduces the costs associated with having expensive high street stores. However, catalogues can be expensive to produce and are not environmentally friendly; they might not fit in with having the aim of being socially responsible. The customer receives no personal attention from the organisation and the time they might have to wait to receive their order might also put them off.

TV shopping channels are another example of direct selling.

? Questions

1. Describe 'channels of distribution'.
2. Suggest factors to take into account when deciding on which channel of distribution to use.
3. Distinguish between a wholesaler and a retailer.
4. Suggest two advantages and two disadvantages of using a wholesaler.
5. Suggest two advantages and two disadvantages of using a retailer.
6. Describe different types of retailers.
7. Give examples of different types of retailers.
8. Define the term 'logistics'.
9. Describe the methods of direct selling.
10. For each method given in Q9, suggest two benefits and two costs of that method.

🔆 Revision activity

Download and complete revision sheet 10 from the Leckie & Leckie website. This looks at methods of promotion.

Promotion

Promotion lets people know that a product exists and tries to encourage them to buy it. This is important because customers need to be informed that a product is available. Advertising is a part of promotion but it isn't the only part of it.

Above and below the line

Promotion is often described as above or below the line.

- **Above the line promotion** – mass media promotions to a large range of people, for example, through newspapers, posters, TV and cinema adverts, radio advertising, billboards and other forms of mass media advertising.

- **Below the line promotion** – promotions to focused groups of people, for example, sales promotions, public relations and direct selling.

Above the line promotion

At National 5, various forms of above the line promotions were covered and you should go back and revise these carefully. Make sure you are able to describe different methods as well as being able to explain the advantages and disadvantages of each. *These are all thoroughly covered in the National 5 Course Notes.* Technology is playing a major role in above the line promotions through, for example, internet websites, social media, e-mail and mobile applications.

Celebrities might also be used to promote a business. This is known as **celebrity** or **product endorsement**.

> ⚠ **Watch point**
>
> You will be asked about the role of technology in marketing in your assessments.

Advantages	Disadvantages
• Promotes a good image and name for the organisation. • People often want to buy products to be associated with the celebrity. • If the celebrity is successful, it can increase sales levels.	• Celebrities are expensive to pay. • The celebrity has to be carefully chosen to match the image the product needs to have. • Negative publicity about the celebrity can impact negatively on sales of the product.

Below the line promotion

Special offers or sales promotions might include discounts on buying a product, free samples or a free gift when you purchase something. They are usually on offer for a limited period of time and try to encourage people to buy the product. For example, magazines usually away free gifts away when they are first launched as well as being at a reduced price to encourage people to buy them. Loyalty cards are another example of sales promotions.

Public relations (PR) attempts to improve the relationship and communication between the general public and an organisation. Large organisations may have a PR office or department that has responsibility for organising different PR events. Effective PR will give the organisation a good image which in turn can increase sales. PR activities include:

Press releases	A press release is usually a written statement to the press (eg newspapers and TV stations) that communicates activities within the organisation.
Sponsorships	Organisations may sponsor events where there is likely to be a lot of public attention. Sport and charity events are often sponsored by large organisations which have their company name displayed on material that the sport or charity is distributing. Football strips sponsored by companies are a good example.
Charity donations	Organisations may donate sums of money to charities in the hope of not only helping a good cause, but also being seen as socially responsible. This will raise awareness of the organisation.

Into and out of the pipeline

Manufacturer

Into the pipeline

Retailers encourage customers to buy from them, for example, free samples, loyalty schemes, credit facilities, demonstrations, competitions, offers such as BOGOF and vouchers

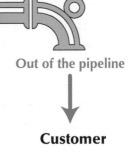

Retailer

Manufacturers encourage retailers to stock their products, for example, point of sale materials, dealer loaders, sale or return, competitions, staff training and credit facilities.

Out of the pipeline

Customer

Into the pipeline promotions	Out of the pipeline promotions
Point of sale materials Often free posters, display standards and other material are given to retailers to display products to customers.	**Free samples** Customers are given small samples of the product free of charge so that they can see/test the product in the hope they will buy it.
Sale or return The manufacturer gives the retailer the opportunity to return products to reduce the risk of being stuck with stock that has not sold.	**Loyalty schemes** Many larger retailers offer loyalty schemes to customers whereby they collect points for making purchases. These points can then be used to obtain vouchers for discount on future purchases or for free admission/discounts for visitor attractions.
Staff training The manufacturer may provide training and demonstrations to the retailer's staff so that they feel confident in promoting the manufacturer's product.	**Vouchers** These are usually given in newspapers/magazines in store. They entitle the customer to a discount on purchases they make at a later date.
Dealer (retailer) loaders These are offers given to encourage the retailer to stock the manufacturer's products (eg buy so many and get one free).	**Special offers** For example, buy one get one free (BOGOF) and other reductions in the price of a product. They are usually short-term and only on selected products.

Marketing and ethics

The **Advertising Standards Authority** monitors advertising and other forms of promotion to ensure they are to the required standard. They also investigate any advertising-related complaints. They have the authority to enforce changes to adverts or promotions if they contain wrong or misleading information.

? Questions

1. Distinguish between above and below the line promotions.
2. Distinguish between into and out of the pipeline promotions.
3. Describe two methods each of above and below the line promotions.
4. For each method given in Q3, suggest two advantages and two disadvantages.
5. Describe two methods each of into and out of the pipeline promotions.
6. For each method given in Q5, suggest two advantages and two disadvantages.
7. Describe the role of public relations.
8. Describe methods of public relations.
9. Suggest ways technology can be used in promotional activities.

★ Key questions

1. Describe and justify each element of the extended marketing mix.
2. Describe methods of carrying out market research.
3. Describe the advantages and disadvantages of having a varied product portfolio.
4. Compare market-led and product-led organisations.
5. Discuss ways technology can be used to help the marketing function.

Summary

This chapter provided you with an overview of the main components of the extended marketing mix, the importance of the customer and various ways market research can be carried out. It also looked at the role of technology in marketing.

The learning intentions for this chapter were:

- Customers
- Market research
- Marketing mix

By successfully answering the key questions, you will have proved that you have grasped the main topics covered in this chapter.

7 Management of Operations

What you will learn about in this chapter:

- Stock management.
- Methods of production.
- Quality.
- Ethical and environmental.
- Technology and operations.

Stock management

The term stock refers to raw materials, goods that are currently being manufactured (work in progress) and finished goods. At all stages of the production process stock must be managed because there must be sufficient quantities of raw materials and finished goods at all times.

At National 5, we explored what factors would be taken into account when choosing a supplier. You should go back and revise this carefully if you need to.

When manufacturing and storing goods there are different factors to consider:

- The quantity of the product that is required.

- The volume of products that can be manufactured at any one time.

- Working practices, procedures and health and safety requirements.

- The storage available in a warehouse.

- Procedures for maintaining and managing quality.

Organisations need to calculate the **optimum** or **economic stock level**. This is the most suitable quantity of stock at any one time. This ensures that costs are kept to a minimum as well as having enough stock to meet production requirements. The purpose of a stock management system is to:

- Ensure stock is readily available at any one time.

- Ensure production continues.

- Avoid delays to customer orders.

- Ensure over-stocking does not take place, which results in higher costs.

- Avoid stock deteriorating (eg fresh food) and/or becoming obsolete.

There are consequences of holding too little or too much stock.

Consequences of too little stock	Consequences of too much stock
• Production could stop and therefore employees and machines sit idle. • Customers might not receive their orders on time, which could result in complaints. • The business could gain a poor reputation and image.	• Increased financial costs (eg storage, security and insurance). • Stock could go to waste or deteriorate, resulting in stock that needs to be discarded. • Higher risk of stock being stolen.

Organisations need to have in place a stock management system to manage stock levels. A stock management system has the following features:

- **Maximum stock level** – the highest amount of stock that can be stored at one time. At this level stock costs will be at the minimum per unit because the organisation is at full capacity.

- **Minimum stock level** – the lowest amount of stock that should be stored at one time. At this level there is a danger that stock levels could fall too low and production would stop.

- **Re-order level** – the quantity at which more stock is ordered.

- **Re-order quantity** – the quantity of stock that has to be ordered to bring levels back to the maximum stock level.

- **Lead time** – the time that passes between ordering stock and it arriving.

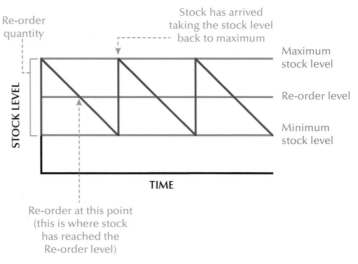

The diagram shows a stock management system in action.

Just in time (JIT)

Just in time (JIT) is a method of stock control that keeps cost levels to the minimum. As the name suggest, stock arrives *just in time* for it to be used in the production process and goods are only manufactured when a customer order is received.

The benefits of a JIT system are:

- Less cash is tied up in stock.

- Less storage and warehouse space is required.

- Wastage should be reduced as only stock required is ordered.

- Changes in the external environment (eg fashion trends) will have a reduced impact.

The costs of a JIT system are:

- Suppliers who are reliable are required so that stock is delivered on time.

- Production can stop if stock is not delivered when required.

- Less environmentally friendly as more journeys with less stock will be made.

- Delivery costs might be higher due to more journeys.

- Discounts for bulk buying (economies of scale) might be lost.

Storage and warehousing

Stock can be stored in a centralised or decentralised location.

- **Centralised storage** – storing stock in one place.

- **Decentralised storage** – storing stock in more than one place.

Centralisation	
Advantages	Disadvantages
• Maintaining security is easier in one location rather than several. • Procedures for receiving, issuing and distributing stock are easier to implement consistently across the organisation.	• A dedicated central area for storing stock could be expensive to set up and maintain. • Staff could waste time going to and from the centralised storage area (it might be some distance from their normal location).

Decentralisation	
Advantages	Disadvantages
• Staff can access stock more easily rather than having to go to a centralised area. • Less chance of stock going to waste or deteriorating.	• Storage space in several locations is required. • Security is more difficult to maintain across a number of locations compared to one (and might also be more expensive).

Warehousing

A warehouse is the name given to the place where finished products are held until they are ready to be distributed to the customer. Warehouses need to be designed to ensure the most efficient movement and flow of stock. The exact size and layout of a warehouse depends on the size of the organisation, the product being manufactured and the organisation's policy for logistics and distribution.

⚬∴ Make the link

A warehouse is part of the channel of distribution.

Distribution and logistics

Distribution and logistics is concerned with getting the finished product to the right customer. Channels of distribution were covered earlier (see page 144) and methods of physical distribution were covered at National 5.

How the product gets to the customer depends on the distribution mix. Some organisations may choose to transport the product themselves or they may employ a company that specialises in logistics and distribution to do this. The distribution mix identifies various factors to be considered when deciding upon the route to get the product to the customer.

Factors to consider

- Reliability of other organisations.

- Legal restrictions.

- Availability of finance.

- The product being distributed.

- The image associated with the product.

- The stock management system being used.

- The distribution capability of the manufacturer.

❓ Questions

1. Describe factors to be considered when selecting a supplier.
2. What is the purpose of a stock management system? Try to include at least four features.
3. Discuss the consequences of having too much stock.
4. Discuss the consequences of having too little stock.
5. Describe the features of a stock management system.
6. Compare centralised and decentralised storage.
7. Describe the features of a JIT system.
8. Describe the advantages and disadvantages of a JIT system.
9. What is a warehouse?
10. Define the term 'logistics'.
11. Suggest factors to be considered when deciding on how to get the product to the customer.

Methods of production

Businesses have to decide which method of production to use to make their products. They have to think carefully about how to actually turn their inputs into outputs.

When deciding which method to use, there are different factors to think about:

- The actual product being made.
- The quantity of the product that needs to be made.
- The way the business will make sure the product is of a high quality.
- The way stock is managed.
- The resources available (eg staff and machinery).
- The method of distribution.
- The technology available.

There are three main methods of production: **job, batch** and **flow**.

> ### ✴️ Make the link
>
> Value is being added to each product as it moves from one stage of production to another.

Job production

Job production is when one product is made from start to finish before another one is made. The product is made to the customer's own requirements and this results in a unique or one-off product being made. Products made by job production are usually made by hand by someone who is very skilled at what they are doing.

Examples: wedding cakes, handmade chocolates, pieces of art, sandwich being made to order in a sandwich shop.

Advantages	Disadvantages
• The customer gets exactly what they want and this can increase their satisfaction. • High prices can often be charged because it is a unique/one-off product. • Designs can be changed to suit each customer's own requirements even when production has begun. • Employees experience making a range of products using different skills. • Employees can be motivated by seeing the product being made from start to finish.	• Highly skilled employees are required to make each different product and this can be expensive (labour intensive). • Specialist tools and equipment might be needed that can be expensive to buy. • Can't always buy raw materials in bulk and might miss out on cost savings from bulk buying (economies of scale). • Can take a long time to make a unique product and this might mean the employee loses motivation.

> ### ⚠ Watch point
>
> Make sure you can describe different methods of production, including advantages and disadvantages of each.

Batch production

Batch production is when one group of identical products are made at any one time. All products in the batch move onto the next stage of production at the same time. Machinery and equipment can be cleaned and/or changed between batches to produce a different product. Batch production is often used when manufacturing a product that comes in different varieties, styles or sizes.

Examples: cakes, newspapers/magazines, bread.

Advantages	Disadvantages
• Batches can be changed to suit the requirements of the customer which results in higher customer satisfaction. • Raw materials can be bought in bulk therefore saving money. • Cost savings can be made, as standardised machinery is used. • The need for highly skilled workers is reduced.	• Equipment and employees might not have anything to do between batches, which costs money. • Any mistakes in one item can result in the whole batch being wasted, which costs money and wastes time. • The cost of each item might be high if the batch size is small therefore the price charged to the customer might be higher. • Employee motivation can be less than with job production, as they carry out the same, often repetitive, task.

Flow production

Flow production (sometimes known as line production) is when parts are added to the product as it moves along the production line. The final product will have been made by the time it reaches the end of the production line. As the product moves along the production line, machinery and workers have very specific tasks to do: one might screw something in and one might paint a very specific part before moving on to the next task (this is known as **division of labour**).

Examples: cars/vans, computers and other electrical items.

Advantages	Disadvantages
• Large amounts of identical products are made. • Raw materials can be bought in bulk, saving the business money. • Production often uses lots of machinery (capital intensive) that, compared to humans, can work for longer and without breaks. • Quality can be easily checked at different stages of production.	• The individual customer's requirements cannot be met because each product is identical. • If a fault occurs during production this can cause the whole production line to stop. • Large demand for products is needed because they are made in large quantities. • Motivation can be low among employees due to the repetitive nature of the work they have to do.

Capital and labour intensive

The quantity of capital (machinery, equipment and technology) or labour used in an organisation determines whether it is **capital** or **labour** intensive.

- **Automation** means that capital has replaced the need for humans to carry out the work required because machines, equipment and technology can do it instead.

- **Mechanisation** means that there is some capital as well as some labour involved in production, eg people working the machines.

Labour intensive	
Advantages	Disadvantages
<ul><li>Employees can use their initiative when required.</li><li>There is always a supply of labour available (though highly skilled employees might be more difficult to source).</li><li>Cheaper than purchasing and maintaining equipment.</li></ul>	<ul><li>It costs money to recruit, select and train new employees.</li><li>The accuracy and the quality of work from person to person can vary.</li></ul>

Capital intensive	
Advantages	Disadvantages
<ul><li>Machines can work 24/7 without the need for breaks.</li><li>Machines can produce a consistent and standardised accuracy and quality of work.</li></ul>	<ul><li>Individual customer requirements cannot be met.</li><li>Breakdowns can occur which can be expensive.</li><li>Employees become tired and bored of repetitive tasks that might need to be carried out.</li></ul>

GO! Paired or group activity

Think of a product that is made using job, batch or flow production. Do some research to find out why it is made in this way and the benefits that this has. Try to find out how much labour and capital is used in the production process. Put your findings into a discussion forum that your teacher has set up.

Skills

- Research
- Thinking
- ICT

? Questions

1. Describe three methods of production.
2. Give an example of each method of production.
3. Suggest advantages and disadvantages of each method of production.
4. Compare labour and capital intensive production.
5. Suggest advantages and disadvantages of labour intensive production.
6. Suggest advantages and disadvantages of capital intensive production.
7. Define the term 'mechanisation'.
8. Define the term 'automation'.

☀ Revision activity

Download and complete revision sheet 12 from the Leckie & Leckie website. This looks at reasons why quality is important and some methods that can be used to ensure quality.

Quality

At National 5, we explored the advantages of providing a high quality product as well as some of the methods that can be used to produce a high quality product. At Higher, you need to know about some different methods of ensuring quality:

- quality standards and symbols
- benchmarking
- quality circles
- mystery shopping

Quality standards and symbols

Quality standards are awarded to an organisation when it meets a particular specification or set of criteria. However, it can be a time-consuming process to achieve and involves a series of checks and/or audits to be carried out. Being awarded a quality standard (or symbol) has benefits to the organisation and the customer.

The organisation benefits from:

- Having a recognised symbol attached to its name, which improves the image and reputation of the product.
- Having proof that it has met specific quality standards.
- Having a competitive advantage over products that do not have a quality standard, which can be used in marketing and promotional material.
- Help to encourage repeat purchases.
- Being able to charge higher prices.
- Receiving fewer complaints and reduced wastage.

Benchmarking

Benchmarking involves comparing one product with another similar product, often using the market leader's standards as the benchmark. The organisation will then attempt to match these standards in their own products.

Quality circles

A quality circle is established when members of the organisation meet to discuss quality issues and then attempt to improve these and find solutions to quality issues. It involves employees at all levels of the hierarchy, which can be motivating.

Mystery shopping

Some organisations, often in retail, employ mystery shoppers to visit their store to make a purchase. Feedback is then given to the organisation on how the shopper found their experience and the service that they received. Staff in the organisation will not normally know in advance that a mystery shopper will be visiting, in an attempt to provide an accurate representation of the shop and the service experienced.

Ethical and environmental

All businesses have to consider environmental and ethical issues. The Government has put in place strict policies and laws that dictate some of the ways businesses have to consider the environment.

Businesses can:

- Try to **minimise wastage** by ensuring employees are trained, ensuring machinery is kept in good condition and by not overstocking. However, providing training and maintaining machinery could be expensive. This would reduce the company's profitability. It is important in maintaining a good reputation that businesses do not simply 'dump' waste materials that could harm the environment, or send all their waste to landfill. They have to make sure that they reduce the amount of waste that is produced as well as ensuring they dispose of it in an environmentally friendly way. Sometimes a business might call on the services of a specialist waste disposal company to dispose of certain types of waste.

- **Recycle as much as possible** by encouraging employees to put rubbish in appropriately coloured bins and by re-using materials in the production process as much as possible. Initially buying the different coloured recycling bins could be expensive, but would hopefully encourage people to recycle as much as they can. Recycling can help reduce the company's energy bill by re-using materials rather than using new ones. Recycling will also help to reduce greenhouse gases by not having to extract new raw materials and by reducing materials that need to be transported.

- **Try to minimise packaging** by only using the amount of packaging needed to maintain the product's quality. Not only will this cut down on costs, it is good for the environment. They also need to try and use as much environmentally friendly packaging that can be recycled as possible; however, it might be more expensive than non-recyclable packaging. Many products that previously had significant amounts of packaging (eg Easter eggs) now contain much less.

- **Prevent pollution and emissions** by watching the materials used in production (eg fuel and chemicals) and by disposing of any potentially harmful chemicals or products in the most environmentally friendly way. Careful disposal of waste can be expensive, but businesses that don't consider this properly can be prosecuted. Businesses also need to be aware of traffic congestion/pollution getting to and from the business, as well as the noise and light that it emits from its premises.

- **Be sustainable** by replacing raw materials that they have used with new ones. For example, toilet paper manufacturers might plant a new tree for every one that they use to make their product. They might have a sustainable development policy that details what the organisation will do to replace materials that it consumes.

- **Operate a fair trade policy,** which means they only use suppliers that have produced or obtained their raw materials in an ethical manner. The fair trade symbol that is on fair trade products means that those who have produced the product (eg farmers) have received a fair price for their product. In addition, the supplier will treat their employees fairly and will have a commitment towards their welfare and health and safety. The fair trade symbol is owned by Fairtrade International and is an independent assurance that the organisation is adopting a fair trade approach to business.

⚬ Make the link

Ethical and environmental issues are related to the objective of social responsibility.

- Ensure animals that are used as part of the product (eg eggs) are given a **high standard of animal welfare**. It might also mean that products (eg cosmetics) are not tested on animals before they are sold to consumers.

- **Use renewable energy sources** rather than ones that cannot be renewed. This will reduce the impact on the environment.

- **Provide information** on the product that will help consumers make decisions, eg nutritional information.

- Adopt **other energy saving strategies** such as energy saving light bulbs, using rain water to flush toilets and solar panels for generating electricity.

GO! Paired activity

Visit the Green Choices website (www.greenchoices.org) to find out what you can do to reduce the impact of your daily life on the environment. Try also to think about what businesses could do to reduce their impact.
Be prepared to feed back to the rest of your class.

⚥ Skills

- Thinking
- ICT
- Decision-making

GO! Group activity

Choose an organisation and investigate what strategies it has adopted to reduce the impact it has on the environment. With your findings, prepare a short presentation that provides:

- Some background information on the organisation and what it does.
- Details of how the organisation is protecting the environment.
- The advantages and disadvantages of the strategies it is adopting to protect the environment.
- Recommendations on what the organisation could do to become even more environmentally friendly.

Be prepared to present your findings to the rest of the class.

⚥ Skills

- Thinking
- ICT
- Decision-making
- Communication

Case study

First Group Plc

First Group Plc is committed to protecting the environment. It is the leading transport company in the UK and provides bus and rail services across the country. It has a number of initiatives in place to reduce wastage, increase recycling and protect the environment. It has a section on its website dedicated to corporate social responsibility and ethics.

In 2012, First Group Plc scrapped over 400 buses. Instead of simply sending these to landfill sites, it tried to recycle as many parts as possible. For example, it tried to reuse engines and gearboxes after they had been reconditioned. This required a close relationship between First Group Plc and its suppliers.

First Group Plc works with the Salvation Army Trading Company to recycle old uniforms. The Salvation Army Trading Company can sell these to raise income for their charity.

The number of train timetables printed, and the size of these, has been reduced to decrease the volume of emissions from printing and also to limit the volume of paper required to print them. First Group Plc is also encouraging customers to print their own timetables directly from the First Group Plc website.

First Group Plc has a supplier code of conduct that lays down the expectations of its suppliers in terms of their environmental responsibilities.

? Questions

1. Suggest reasons why First Group Plc is committed to protecting the environment.
2. From the case study, identify ways that First Group Plc is protecting the environment.
3. For each way identified in Q2, discuss how it would reduce the impact on the environment.

Technology and operations

Technology can be used in a number of different ways in the operations function.

- Computer facilities (eg computer and internet) can be used for purchasing materials online.

- E-mail can be used to confirm an order has been received and to let the customer know about the progress and status of the order (eg when it has been dispatched).

- Websites can be used to compare the prices of different suppliers before deciding which one to purchase.

- Deliveries can be tracked and traced via the websites of logistical companies.

- Computer programs (eg a database or spreadsheet) can be used to store stock levels.

- EPOS (see page 129) can provide automatic updates on stock and sales levels.

- Computer-aided design (CAD) can be used in the research and design stage of a new product before it is manufactured.

- Computer-aided manufacture (CAM) involves using computer-controlled equipment and robots in the manufacturing of a product (eg automation).

⚠ Watch point

Be able to give examples of when technology could be used in operations.

? Questions

1. Describe the following methods of maintaining quality:

   - quality control
   - quality assurance
   - quality management
   - benchmarking
   - mystery shopping
   - quality symbols

2. Justify the use of each method.
3. Describe the features of fair trade.
4. Describe methods that a business could adopt to protect the environment.
5. Suggest an advantage and a disadvantage of each method given in Q4.
6. Compare CAD and CAM.
7. Describe ways technology could be used in the stock management process.

★ Key questions

1. Describe the features of a stock management system.
2. Describe methods of production.
3. Compare labour and capital intensive.
4. Describe and justify methods of ensuring quality.
5. Discuss environmental and ethical issues to be considered by a business.
6. Describe how technology could support the operations function.

Summary

This chapter provided you with an overview of how stock can be managed, different methods of production and ways businesses can ensure quality. Environmental and ethical issues were explored, as was the role of technology in operations.

The learning intentions for this chapter were:

- Stock management
- Methods of production
- Quality
- Ethical and environmental
- Technology and operations

By successfully answering the key questions, you will have proved that you have grasped the main topics covered in this chapter.

3 END OF UNIT MATERIAL

Unit Assessment

To pass the Unit Assessment, you have to achieve each Assessment Standard. For this Unit, the Learning Outcomes and Assessment Standards are:

Outcome 1: Apply knowledge and understanding of how the marketing function enhances the effectiveness of large organisations by:

- Explaining how market research can be used to enhance the effectiveness of large organisations.

- Explaining how the marketing mix can be used to enhance the effectiveness of large organisations.

- Describing the costs and benefits to large organisations of having varied product portfolios.

- Describing how current technologies are used in the marketing function.

Outcome 2: Apply knowledge and understanding of how the operations function contributes to the success of large organisations by:

- Describing the features and outlining the purposes of a stock management control system.

- Explaining methods that can be used to ensure customers receive quality products/services.

- Explaining the costs and benefits of contemporary production methods used by large organisations.

- Describing how current technologies are used in the operations function.

Your teacher will make sure you know what you have to do to pass each Unit.

> ⚠ **Watch point**
>
> The Outcomes and Assessment Standards give you an indication of the things that will come up in your Unit Assessment.

Exam questions: Management of Marketing and Operations

- Discuss methods of ensuring quality. (6 marks)

Make sure you read the question carefully as every word is there for a reason. It is good practice to break the question down into parts before you start to answer it – this will make sure you answer it as best you can.

Discuss methods of ensuring quality. (6 marks)

> The command word – your instruction on how to answer the question.

> Plural – so more than one method (also remember it is worth 6 marks).

Sample answer

An organisation can ensure quality in a number of different ways. It could use quality assurance, which is when products are checked at different stages of production. (**1 mark**) This allows any problems to be identified as early as possible to reduce the possible number of products that might go to waste. (**1 mark**) It could also use quality control, which is when a check takes place at the end of production. (**1 mark**) Benchmarking is another method, which is when the organisation attempts to produce a product that matches, or exceeds, the standard of the market-leading product. (**1 mark**) Finally, quality circles could be used, where members of the organisation get together to discuss quality issues. (**1 mark**) This can be motivating to those involved as they are involved in finding solutions to quality problems. (**1 mark**)

Examiner's commentary

The candidate has discussed four ways of ensuring quality. No marks were awarded for naming the method (as the question was not to identify). (**6/6**)

Further questions for you to try

- Describe the purpose of marketing activities. (3 marks)
- Describe and justify elements of the extended marketing mix. (6 marks)
- Explain how technology could enhance the marketing function. (6 marks)
- Explain how technology could enhance the operations function. (6 marks)
- Suggest reasons why organisations carry out market research. (4 marks)
- Describe methods of field research. (5 marks)
- Compare methods of sampling. (2 marks)
- Describe into and out of the pipeline promotions. (6 marks)
- Describe levels of profitability that would be achieved at each stage of the product life cycle. (6 marks)
- Explain benefits of having a varied product portfolio. (4 marks)
- Compare labour and capital intensive production. (3 marks)

- Discuss issues surrounding marketing ethically. (5 marks)
- Describe environmental issues an organisation needs to consider. (6 marks)
- Describe and justify methods of production. (6 marks)
- Explain the benefits and costs of batch production. (4 marks)
- Explain the benefits and costs of flow production. (4 marks)
- Define the terms 'automation' and 'mechanisation'. (2 marks)
- Describe how an organisation could implement a stock management system. (6 marks)

Check your progress

	HELP NEEDED	GETTING THERE	CONFIDENT
Market segmentation	◯	◯	◯
Consumer behaviour	◯	◯	◯
Desk research	◯	◯	◯
Field research	◯	◯	◯
Product, life cycle, extension strategies	◯	◯	◯
Pricing strategies	◯	◯	◯
Place, channels of distribution, retailers and wholesalers	◯	◯	◯
Promotion, methods of promotion	◯	◯	◯
Process	◯	◯	◯
People	◯	◯	◯
Physical evidence	◯	◯	◯

	HELP NEEDED	GETTING THERE	CONFIDENT
Sampling	◯	◯	◯
Technology and marketing	◯	◯	◯
Stock management, systems, storage, JIT	◯	◯	◯
Methods of production	◯	◯	◯
Ensuring quality	◯	◯	◯
Logistics and distribution	◯	◯	◯
Environmental and ethical issues	◯	◯	◯
Technology and operations	◯	◯	◯

What actions do you need to take to improve your knowledge?

Case study answers

Primark case study (page 28)

1. Behaving in a responsible way and/or protecting the environment.

2. To provide affordable and fashionable clothes.

3. To summarise its commitment to corporate social responsibility.

4. Taking care of our people, respecting our neighbours and fostering ethical business relationships.

5. A set of standards to be complied with.

6. By conducting regular visits to its suppliers.

7. Costly to implement (eg Primark conducts visits to ensure it is being followed – this will cost money).

The International Airlines Group (IAG) case study (page 33)

1. To increase sales and profit, to increase market share, to obtain economies of scale, to prevent risk of a takeover, to gain a better reputation.

2. Two businesses agree to become one.

3. Vertical integration.

4. To reduce competition, to obtain economies of scale, to grow (become market leader), to be able to charge higher prices due to fewer competitors.

Morrisons case study (page 34)

1. Market share – number of customers/sales revenue generated from a market. Market growth – an increase in the number of customers/sales revenue in a market.

2. To increase sales and profit, which in turn will increase the return on investment for owners (eg dividends for shareholders). To increase the number of customers, which will increase profits and market share, and may enable the organisation to become a market leader. To take advantage of economies of scale (discounts for bulk buying), therefore reducing costs. To become bigger with the intention that it will reduce risk of a takeover by another organisation. To gain a better reputation in the marketplace which will encourage new customers to buy, therefore increasing sales and ultimately profit.

3. Backward vertical integration – eg purchasing farms and Flower World – buying a supplier. Organic growth – increasing the number of outlets, eg Morrisons convenience stores. Diversification – beginning to operate in a new market, eg Kiddicare.

4. Dependent on answers given in Q3.

5. By sourcing food from its own suppliers, commitment to waste reduction, working with schools and charity partnerships.

6. To gain a good reputation/image, to increase the number of customers/sales, to gain positive media attention.

Premier Inn case study (page 68)

1. Environmental and technological.

2. Some examples: Premier Inn needs its employees to implement the Greener Together initiative and its employees need Premier Inn to provide training. Premier Inn needs its suppliers to supply sustainable paper at reasonable prices and its suppliers need Premier Inn to purchase from them. Premier Inn needs its suppliers to find ways of reducing wastage and suppliers need Premier Inn to invest in these methods.

3. Some examples: Premier Inn wants to keep costs low by encouraging customers to recycle their towels etc, whereas its customers want to take advantage of the fact they are staying in a hotel. Shareholders (as it is a plc) want a high return on their investment whereas customers want value for money.

4. Having the UK's greenest and eco-friendliest hotel, using cutting-edge technology.

5. It will receive positive media attention, it can use this as part of an advertising campaign, it will encourage customers, it can contribute towards achieving the aim of social responsibility.

6. Organic growth – growing internally by increasing the number of rooms/hotels it has.

First Group Plc case study (page 167)

1. To meet its aim of being socially responsible, to gain a good image/reputation, to gain positive media attention, to increase sales.

2. Reusing parts from buses rather than sending to landfill, recycling old uniforms, reducing the number of timetables it is producing, encouraging customers to print their own timetables.

3. Reusing parts from buses - cuts down on the volume of parts being sent to landfill and the number of journeys that would need to be made to take old buses to landfill. Recycling old uniforms – saves energy being used in disposing of these and/or decreases volume being sent to landfill. Also shows a social commitment towards the charity. Reducing the number of timetables it is producing – reduction in volume to be transported (reduces carbon emissions), reduction in paper being used in production, reduction in energy needed to produce timetables. Also reduces costs (and therefore increases profitability). Encouraging customers to print their own timetables – reduces costs to First Group and also the volume of timetables it needs to produce.

Answers to questions

Unit 1 : Understanding Business

PAGE 16

1. Primary – businesses in the primary sector extract raw materials from the ground. These businesses include agriculture, fishing, oil and gas extraction, and mining.

    Secondary – businesses in this sector manufacture goods. They take raw materials and transform them into a tangible, finished product. Examples include shipbuilding, breweries and builders.

    Tertiary – businesses in the tertiary sector provide a service, an intangible product. The service is provided by people who have been trained to offer it. Examples include fitness instructors, hotels, supermarkets, hairdressers and health care providers.

    Quaternary – businesses in the quaternary sector provide a knowledge-based and information service and are often concerned with innovation, research and development. This includes consultancy, ICT and computing, education, scientific research and financial services. People working in the quaternary sector are highly skilled.

2. Wealth is created by a business by adding value to a product as it goes through the production process.

3. Gross domestic product – the value of all the goods and services produced in the UK.

4. **Advantages**
    *   Jobs are created and therefore this reduces the UK's unemployment figure.
    *   When people become employed, they might have access to training and the opportunity to learn new skills.
    *   As a result of less unemployment, demand for goods and services increases and the standard of living increases.
    *   Tax is paid by businesses and individuals when they have a job and this money is paid to the Government that can then invest this money into different Government services eg health, police and education.
    *   Other businesses will be keen to invest.
    *   Infrastructure (eg access to utilities such as water and electricity) can be improved and roads and transport links can be improved.

    Disadvantages
    *   Businesses can have a large environmental impact on a country or specific location (eg noise and traffic pollution or an increase in wastage).
    *   The volume of non-renewable resources, eg oil, can decrease.
    *   Greenfield sites, land that has previously been unused or used for agriculture, is lost – however, this could be seen as an advantage.
    *   Too much demand for goods and services can cause inflation; this is when the price of goods and services rises and people may no longer be able to afford to purchase some products.

PAGE 25

1. Private limited company shareholders have to be invited to become shareholders whereas with a public limited company, shares are available to anyone in the stock market. Both are private sector businesses.

2. **Advantages**

    - Limited liability for the shareholders of the company (this means if the company was to go bankrupt, shareholders would only lose the money they invested into the company and not their own personal assets). This also means that shareholders may be more likely to invest in the company.
    - Large amounts of capital (finance) can be raised by selling more shares via the stock exchange and lenders may feel more confident in investing in larger companies.
    - Can often take advantage of economies of scale because of their size; this means they can obtain discounts for buying in bulk eg raw materials.
    - Plcs can control more of the market compared to smaller organisations and therefore have more power within it.

    Disadvantages

    - Financial statements have to be published annually that will involve a cost in producing them.
    - There is no control over who can buy shares in the company.
    - Company has to abide by the Company Act to avoid legal action being taken.
    - Profits may be lower when the company is initially set up due to high start up costs.

3. A person who starts a business and provides a good or service supplied by another business (the franchisor) is known as a franchisee and operates a business known as a franchise.

4. **Advantages:**

    - Income is guaranteed as the franchisee normally pays a percentage of profit each year to the franchisor.
    - If the business does not work, the cost of failure is split and therefore risk is shared.
    - Market share of the whole franchise is increasing when more branches are being opened.

    Disadvantages

    - As only a percentage of turnover is given to the franchisor by the franchisee, this might be lower than what the franchisor could have earned themselves.
    - A franchisee could damage the reputation and image of the business and this could cause problems for the whole franchise.

5. **Advantages:**

    - They can set up a business using a business name that is well established and that people are familiar with. This could allow them to gain customers and sales quickly compared to setting up a brand new business. It also reduces the risk of failure.
    - Advertising costs are paid for by the franchisor which saves the franchisee having to spend money on this themselves.
    - Franchisor carries out training for the whole business and therefore it is appropriate to the needs of the workforce and will save the franchisee money.

Disadvantages:

- It requires a considerable sum of money to set up a franchise and the franchisee may not have this money available.
- The franchisee might have little or no control over the products available, their price or the layout of the store. The franchisee might find this frustrating as they cannot inject any new ideas into the business.
- Some of the profit earned has to be given to the franchisor therefore reducing the money that the franchisee earns.

6. **Advantages**

- Economies of scale can be taken advantage of therefore reducing costs.
- Legal restrictions can be avoided in other countries compared to the home country.
- May be able to take advantage of different tax regulations in other countries therefore increasing profitability.
- Expanding abroad will mean the organisation becomes bigger, increasing sales and also safer from takeovers by other organisations.
- Government grants might be given in some countries for locating there that do not require to be paid back.
- Resources eg labour, might be cheaper in some countries reducing the overall amount spent on expenses.

Disadvantages

- Each country's laws will need to be complied with – this might mean changes need to be made to the good or service that might be expensive.
- The culture in each country might vary from one to another and the organisation will need to consider this.
- Language barriers may make trading more difficult and expensive if language interpreters need to be employed.
- Language barriers may also mean that communication is misinterpreted and decisions wrongly made.

7. Providing jobs, not polluting the environment (eg recycling what it can), respecting home laws.

8.
- Language differences – trading might be more difficult.
- Cultural differences – different cultures might need to be respected eg customers and employees.
- Cheaper labour – higher profitability, lower expenses.
- Different tax rates – might be lower, resulting in higher profitability.
- Raw materials could be more easily accessed lowering costs.

9. National Government controls what happens in the UK and makes decisions impacting on the whole of the UK. In Scotland, we also have a Scottish Government that has devolved responsibility from the House of Commons for certain things eg education and health. Local governments make decisions and control budgets for the local area eg Glasgow City Council.

10. Third sector businesses:

- Charities are owned and controlled by a Board of Trustees. They are regulated by the Government and the income they make is put towards a specific cause.
- Social Enterprises have a main social or environmental aim rather than to make profit for owners or shareholders, but are run in a business – like way.

PAGE 35

1. Private sector

- To maximise profit
- To satisfy shareholders
- To provide high quality products

Public sector

- To provide a service to communities
- To keep within budgets

Third sector

- To help a specific cause
- To raise donations

All businesses (regardless of sector) might have the objective of being socially responsible.

2. Private sector

- To maximise profit – to ensure dividend payments are made to shareholders.
- To satisfy shareholders – to ensure they continue to invest into the company.
- To provide high quality products – to satisfy customers.

Public sector

- To provide a service to communities – to ensure communities get what they need.
- To keep within budgets – to ensure they break even and don't have a budget deficit.

Third sector

- To help a specific cause eg to relieve poverty or to provide a service to communities.
- To raise donations – to help ensure maximum benefit is given.

3. Horizontal integration – two businesses providing the same service or producing the same good join together (eg two airlines joining together).

When businesses in the same industry, but which operate at different stages of production, join together this is called vertical integration. This cuts out the middle men involved with two separate businesses and therefore cuts costs. There are two types of vertical integration:

- Backward vertical integration – taking over a supplier.
- Forward vertical integration – taking over a customer.

Diversification is when two businesses that provide different goods and services join together. It is also referred to as a conglomerate.

A takeover is when one large business takes control and ownership of a smaller one.

A merger is when two businesses of approximately the same size agree to become one.

Organic growth happens when the business increases the number of goods and services it offers or increases the number of branches/outlets and employees that it has. This will help to increase sales and profit.

Deintegration (or demerger) occurs when a business splits into two or more separate businesses.

Divestment is when a business sells off some of its assets or smaller parts of the business to raise finance.

4. It will reduce risk of failure by operating in more than one market and will also allow profit to be obtained from more than one market.

5. The parts of the business that are sold off are normally less profitable and this finance can be put back into the business.

6. Manager might put their own objectives before the organisation.

7. • To encourage customer loyalty
   • To gain a good reputation

PAGE 40

1. • Size of the organisation (eg larger organisations tend to require a more formal structure compared to smaller ones).
   • The technology being used (eg this could be used to communicate with other parts of the organisations in other locations).
   • Who the customer is (in other words, the target market).
   • The good or service that is being provided.
   • The amount of finance available to the organisation (eg this might limit the type of structure or grouping that could be used).

2. • Who has overall **responsibility** for the organisation.
   • The different levels of **authority** and **responsibility** within the organisation.
   • The lines of **communication** and the **chain of command**.
   • The **span of control** for different managers.
   • Different **relationships** that exist within the organisation.
   • Where work could be **delegated** to **subordinates**.

3. • Delegation – giving the authority and responsibility to someone else to carry out a particular task.
   • Chain of command – this shows how instructions are passed down through an organisation and how communication can flow up and down the organisation.
   • Authority – having power to make decisions.
   • Responsibility – being answerable for decisions and actions taken within the organisation.

4. Human resources, finance, operations, research & development, marketing

5. Comparison of any two structures from page 37-39.

6. • The needs of customers within each specific location can be catered for.
   • The organisation can become familiar with different cultures that exist in different locations.

7. • People can contact specific departments if they require specialist advice or help (eg Marketing might contact HR when recruiting a new employee for that department).
   • Clear lines of authority exist (as shown on the organisation chart) between subordinates
   • Managers and other employees will usually have clearly defined tasks and duties to carry out.

8. Products can be marketed towards each specific customer group. The organisation can build up loyalty with their customers because activities are focused on the specific customer group, and therefore a higher level of customer service is achieved.

PAGE 44

1. Wide span of control means there are many subordinates whereas a narrow span of control means few subordinates.

2. • More empowerment is possible due to the number of subordinates.
   • Tasks can be delegated more easily to the subordinate most suitably skilled to carry these out, however, employees may feel reluctant and uncomfortable with this.
   • As there are a large number of subordinates, this can cause extra stress for the manager who may have little time to deal with staff-related issues.
   • Managers may feel that, as they have more subordinates to manage they are more powerful and this can be motivating to them.
   • The organisation will have fewer managers and therefore save money.
   • A shorter chain of command will exist and therefore communication and decision-making is likely to be more effective.

3. Subordinates are more likely to have the chance to participate in decision-making and planning. However, a long chain of command will exist and therefore communication and decision-making might be slower.

4. A tall structure has many layers/levels whereas a flat structure has fewer. A tall structure has a long chain of command whereas a flat structure has a shorter chain of command.

5. • Matrix (or project-based) structures tend to be formed when a specific task or project is to be carried out.
   • People from across the organisation will come together from various departments to form the matrix structure.
   • When the task or project has been completed, the matrix structure will become obsolete.
   • A project or team leader will be appointed to provide leadership to the task or project being undertaken.
   • Because people from across the organisation may participate in this structure, it can be motivating for employees and useful to the organisation when problems are being solved.
   • Even though it gives employees the opportunity to learn new skills by participating in a project or task, it can be costly to implement and for the organisation to coordinate.
   • Employees may find having two managers (eg from their own functional area as well as for the matrix structure) confusing.

6. **Advantages**
   - Suitable for smaller organisations
   - Decisions can be made quickly by the owner

   Disadvantages
   - Little input from employees, lower motivation
   - Fewer ideas as employees are not consulted

7. Decisions are made by senior management in a centralised structure whereas they are delegated to departments in a decentralised structure. Employees in a centralised structure are consulted whereas in a decentralised structure they are not. Consistency of decision-making exists in a centralised structure whereas in a decentralised structure this cannot always be the case.

8. See notes on page 43.

9. • Line relationship – this is a relationship between a subordinate and their line manager.
   - Lateral relationship – this is a relationship between two or more people on the same level of the organisation.
   - Functional relationship – this is a relationship between two functional areas in an organisation, eg one providing support to another.
   - Staff relationship – this is a relationship between two or more people in an organisation who provide advice or support to others.

10. A formal relationship exists when two people communicate on a formal basis, eg because of a line or lateral relationship within the organisation. An informal relationship is when two or more people communicate on an informal basis, perhaps outwith the organisation, eg over coffee.

PAGE 46

1. • The size of the organisation has changed.
   - The availability of finance has changed.
   - Market conditions have changed.
   - New technology has become available.

2. Delayering involves removing layers of a structure whereas downsizing involves removing some of the activities from an organisation.

3. • As well as saving money on management salaries, it allows for quicker communication and decision-making because there are fewer layers.
   - Market conditions may be responded to more quickly compared to in a taller structure.
   - Employees may feel more empowered to make decisions and to use their own initiative; this can increase motivation and productivity.

4. Employees may feel more empowered to make decisions and to use their own initiative; this can increase motivation and productivity. This is because managers will have a wider span of control. Ultimately, might mean that the supervision and management of employees could be more difficult. Delayering also means that there will be fewer promotion opportunities for existing staff.

5. • To enable the organisation to concentrate on core activities.

    • Specialists may carry out the activity on behalf of the organisation.

PAGE 58

1. • Financial – there might not be enough finance to make new purchases.
    • Employees – employees might not have the correct skills or motivation required to carry out a task.
    • Management – managers might not have enough experience or skill in decision-making.
    • Existing technology – the technology that a business has might not be the best available or suitable to carry out certain tasks.

2. Corporate culture is sometimes referred to as organisational culture. It consists of everything to do with the organisation including its values, emotions, beliefs and the language used. It is also to do with the attitude and behaviours that members of the organisation adopt because of the culture within the organisation.

3. • Employees feel they are part of and belong to the organisation; this can provide them with a sense of security and can improve motivation.
    • It can motivate staff which in turn will lead to improved efficiency and higher productivity.
    • It can create positive relationships within the organisation that will enable better communication and decision-making.
    • Employee loyalty can be increased which will decrease staff turnover and staff absence rates.
    • The image and identity of the organisation can be improved which will be visible to all stakeholders.
    • Customer loyalty might be higher because they associate themselves with the identity (eg logos, uniform and store design) of the organisation. It may also be recognisable across the globe if it is a multinational organisation.
    • There will be consistency across the organisation which will allow employees to work in different locations or branches if necessary.

4. • Strategic – long-term decisions, made by senior management, concerned with the overall direction and focus of the organisation.
    • Tactical – medium-term decisions, made by middle management, concerned with actions to achieve strategic decisions.
    • Operational – short-term decisions, made by junior management, that affect the day-to-day running of the organisation.

5. • Strategic – to expand into a new country, to merge, to diversify the product range.
    • Tactical – to find a cheaper supplier, to expand the range of goods/services, to develop a new marketing strategy.
    • Operational – staff working hours, to give someone a day off.

6.

Identify the problem	Identifying the problem or issue that needs to be resolved by making a decision.
Identify the objectives	What needs to be achieved when making the decision.
Gather information	Gathering information from a variety of resources (primary and secondary) to aid decision-making.
Analyse the information gathered	Looking very carefully at and questioning the quality of the information that has been gathered. (Remember, not all sources of information are of high quality. Look for sources that are reliable, accurate, timely, comprehensive and concise).
Devise possible solutions	Creating a list of possible solutions to the problem or issue in question
Select the best solution	Choosing the best solution from the range of solutions available. There might be internal factors (eg finance, employees and technology) and external factors that impact upon the solution chosen.
Communicate the decision	Letting different stakeholders know of the decision that has been made.
Implement the decision	Taking action to put into practice the solution that has been chosen.
Evaluate the effectiveness of the decision	Considering how successful the decision has been. Changes might need to be made once the decision has been evaluated.

7.
- No quick decisions are made because time is given to gather and then analyse the information; the first option might not be the one that is the best and subsequently implemented.
- Time is given to think about and consider the range of options available; the strengths and weaknesses of each option can be considered to ensure the best decision is made.
- Factors (internal and external) that may impact upon the decision can be considered when time permits and therefore a whole range of information has been considered.
- The effectiveness and impact of each decision is considered during the evaluation stage and, where necessary, changes made to ensure that the decision is the most effective it can be.
- Better ideas might be formulated when following a structured process that will result in a higher quality decision being made.
- The decision will be shared with relevant stakeholders therefore ensuring all those who need to be aware of it are informed.

8. S – strengths, W – weaknesses, O – opportunities, T – threats

9.

Spreadsheets	• Sales forecasts can be made to see what impact a decision might have. • 'What if' scenarios can be created to see what may happen when a decision is made. • Graphs can be created to make comparisons between different options. • Information can be handled more easily and quickly by, for example, using statistics to analyse information.
Databases	• Large amounts of information can be stored, edited, searched and presented using reports.
Word Processing	• Letters can be written, communicating decisions. • Reports can be written, detailing the decision to be made and the options available, and given to managers for consultation.

Presentation Software	• Presentations communicating the decision can be created. • Information can be displayed visually and communicated to a large number of people at a conference or meeting.
The Internet	• Information can be sourced from a number of sources quickly (eg information on competitors can be accessed). • Decisions can be communicated via a website or via a social networking site.
Intranet	• Documents can be shared via an organisation's intranet. • Documents can be updated quickly and shared quickly but only to those within the organisation.
E-mail	• Communication can take place almost at any time or place (especially if using a smart telephone or table computer with internet access).
Videoconferencing	• Meetings can take place over long distances between different branches and offices to discuss decisions.

10. • Asking employees for their views (in other words, obtaining qualitative information) on how well the decision has worked and how effective they think it is.
  • Looking at quantitative information (eg productivity rates and sales or profit figures) to see if the decision has impacted negatively or positively.
  • Looking at employee absence rates (again, quantitative information) to see if there has been an increase or decrease in the number of days employees take off work.
  • Measuring the level of employee motivation within the workplace to see whether or not the decision has reduced or increased this.
  • Asking customers for their opinion by carrying out research (eg conducting a survey) as this will give first-hand information from their opinion.

PAGE 65

1. Things outwith the control of an organisation that impact on how it operates.

2. Any two from each table given on pages 60-64.

3. • Changes to economic policy may increase consumers' buying power, therefore increasing demand for a business.
  • Changes to an economic policy might restrict the ability of banks to lend money and this may cause a cash flow problem.

4. Positive and negative impacts of different environmental influences are given on page 64.

5. • To remain competitive
  • For planning purposes
  • To make decisions
  • To ensure survival
  • To maximise profit

6. • S-commerce – buying and selling through a social networking site.
   • 4G – fourth generation mobile technology that will provide superfast broadband speeds.
   • Web 2.0 – allows people to interact with each other via, for example, social networking.
   • Cloud computing – storing information in the cloud (online).

7. • Try to find an alternative lender that may have cheaper rates.
   • Ensure they also have access to s-commerce by buying and selling via social networking.
   • Carry out market research and then provide customers with the fashion that they want.
   • May have to change location.

Unit 2 : Management of People and Finance

PAGE 78

1. To ensure the organisation has the correct employees in place at the right time to meet organisational needs.

2. • The correct number of employees will be available at the right time who have the appropriate skills.
   • Future staffing levels/requirements will be considered.
   • Changes in the labour market will have been considered.

3. Internal recruitment is recruiting existing staff from within the organisation whereas external recruitment is recruiting staff who don't already work for the organisation.

4.

Advantages	Disadvantages
• Job vacancy can be filled quickly which means the time can be spent on other activities • Employees are already known by the organisation and, if chosen, will have been so because they have demonstrated they have the ability to do the job • Employees feel more valued and can become more motivated and productive if given the chance of promotion • Money can be saved on advertising a job, recruiting, selecting and training, therefore increasing profitability • Existing employees are already familiar with the policies, procedures and culture within the organisation and therefore do not need to be given guidance on this	• The opportunity to gain new ideas from a new employee is lost and this could mean that new solutions to problems are not discovered • An existing employee with the correct skills or ability for the job might not be available, therefore the position may remain unfilled • There might not be that many existing employees that can apply for the position therefore limited candidates to choose from • If a candidate is recruited internally, this will consequentially create another vacancy within the organisation that then needs to be filled (costly and time consuming) • Conflict amongst existing employees competing for the job might exist and this might cause poor working relationships

5.

Advantages	Disadvantages
• People with new ideas can be brought into the organisation that can help enhance the effectiveness of the organisation • Can attract large quantities of applicants so that the organisation has a range of people to choose from (however, this could be a disadvantage as it will be more time consuming to look at large quantities of applications) • Job vacancies can be filled quickly using the help of recruitment agencies meaning quicker productivity from the new employee • Avoids conflict that may arise between competing employees within an organisation if only internal recruitment is used, therefore, better working relationships • Specialist newspapers, magazines and agencies can be used to find appropriate staff, for example, for specialist posts meaning the most suitably qualified people can be targeted	• Existing employees who apply but do not get the job may feel unvalued and therefore lose the motivation to work hard • It can be expensive to advertise a job externally for example, in a national newspaper and is usually a more expensive form of recruitment compared to internal • May require a more thorough selection process, which can be expensive and time consuming, compared to internal recruitment • There is always a chance that the wrong person is chosen as they are unknown to the organisation, despite employing a number of selection methods, which could be costly

6. Newspapers/magazines, recruitment agencies, universities and colleges, recruitment websites, eg S1 Jobs

7. • Internal vacancies could be circulated via e-mail or on the organisation's intranet.
   • Application forms could be completed online.
   • Databases could be populated with the details of people applying which can be used as part of a mail merge when letters are being sent out.
   • Websites could be used to advertise vacancies.

8. • Identifying a job vacancy involves making sure that there is actually a position that needs to be filled.
   • Conducting a job analysis involves looking at the skills, qualities and experience that a person doing the job would need and what tasks they would complete.
   • Preparing a job specification/description involves creating a document containing the duties and responsibilities of the post holder.
   • Preparing a person specification involves creating a document containing the skills, qualities and experience necessary of the post holder, including which ones are essential and which are desirable.

PAGE 82

1. • CV – curriculum vitae, document created by an applicant that contains the information they want to disclose, eg education, employment history.
   • Application form – document created by the organisation that asks questions of the applicant.
   • Reference – a report from a previous employer or school/college.

2. • They allow the organisation to meet applicants, ask them questions and to find out whether or not they are suitable for the job vacancy.
   • They also allow the applicant to ask questions to see whether or not the vacancy is for them.

3.

Advantages	Disadvantages
• Personality and appearance of the applicant is seen so that the organisation can see if they will fit in • The content of the applicant's CV or application form can be checked which means they can be sure the information is accurate • The applicant can ask questions to make sure the job is right for them	• Time consuming to carry out therefore expensive • Some people don't perform well at interviews, but might be suitable for the job so the wrong person could be chosen • Interviewer bias can exist which means the most suitably qualified person might not necessarily be selected

4. One-to-one interviews

One interviewer interviews all of the short-listed applicants and then makes a decision on who to select.

Successive interviews

Several interviewers interview each applicant separately.

Panel interviews

A panel interview involves one applicant being interviewed by several people at one time.

5. • Skills and abilities can be confirmed.
   • Confirmation of what the applicant has said on their application form can be obtained.

6. Any four from the table on page 80.

7. Assessment centres allow an organisation to see a large number of applicants undertaking a variety of tasks in different situations and realistic work-related scenarios.

8. Benefits

   • Large number of applicants can be seen.
   • Different things can be tested eg team working.
   • Can see how well applicants work under pressure.
   • Interviewer bias is reduced.

Costs

   • Expensive to carry out.
   • Requires significant prior preparation.
   • Facilities are required to hold the assessment centre.
   • Several members of staff are needed to conduct the assessment centre.

PAGE 84

1. On-the-job training is training in the workplace whereas off-the-job training is training outwith the workplace eg at a college or training provider.

2. Induction training introduces new members of staff to the organisation and its policies/procedures.

3. Continuing professional development – opportunities to develop as individuals and employees.

4. Benefits

- Jobs can be carried out better.
- Allows customer service to be better.
- Helps to achieve organisational objectives.
- Keep up-to-date with the external business environment.
- Contributes to the Scottish Government's life-long learning agenda.
- Record of training and development kept.

Costs

- Training is expensive.
- Time consuming to participate in development and training activities.
- Productivity is lower when training is being carried out.

5. Virtual learning environment – password-protected website that people can access to obtain training materials.

6. Saves on printing costs and is more environmentally friendly than providing hard copies of training materials. People do not need to travel to participate in training – less pollution.

7.

Advantages	Disadvantages
<ul><li>Can be accessed at any time of the day in any location</li><li>Large numbers of people can access it</li><li>Can be updated easily with notes, tasks, videos and other materials</li><li>Interaction between users can take place through discussion forums and live chat facilities</li></ul>	<ul><li>People need to be self-disciplined to access the facility and carry out the activities</li><li>People may prefer face-to-face contact rather than virtual learning; might not suit their own learning style</li><li>Might be expensive to employ a specialist to set-up and maintain a virtual learning facility</li></ul>

8. To confirm that the person has achieved a certain standard on a work-based qualification.

9.

Advantages	Disadvantages
<ul><li>A recognised qualification can be gained</li><li>Training often takes place on-the-job</li><li>Assessment is carried out by a qualified Assessor</li><li>The organisation benefits from having skilled staff</li></ul>	<ul><li>Time consuming to complete</li><li>Some people might not want to complete a qualification</li><li>Costs money to enter someone for a qualification</li></ul>

10. Someone learns a trade on the job, eg joinery, and may attend a local college to gain a recognised qualification.

PAGE 88

1. Any three from the table on page 85.

2. Motivation theories can be used to understand what motivates people and can be applied in an organisation to motivate people.

3. • Maslow suggested that there are five levels of human needs that can be satisfied.
   • Each level needs to be satisfied before someone can progress to the next level, starting at the bottom of the pyramid.
   • If something is not satisfied at one level, they cannot progress to the next.

4. • Adam's Equity Theory proposes that what people put into their work (inputs) should be matched by appropriate rewards (outputs).
   • When inputs and outputs are the same, people are generally satisfied.
   • However, when inputs are greater than outputs, people become demotivated.

5. Theory X managers believe employees do not like work and try to avoid it, whereas Theory Y managers believe people achieve satisfaction from a job.

6. • Autocratic – authority and power rests with the leader and decisions are made by them.
   • Democratic – consultation and communication with employees is important.
   • Laissez-faire – no control is exercised over employees and people are left to get on with things themselves.

7. **Autocratic**

   • Benefits: standardised decisions across the organisation, tight control, quicker decision-making.
   • Costs: no opportunities to gain ideas from individuals, lack of opportunities for people to learn.

   Democratic

   • Benefits: more opportunities to gain ideas, more opportunities to learn and participate which can be motivating.
   • Costs: lack of standardisation, slower decision-making.

   Laissez-faire

   • Benefits: people are free to get on with things, people can feel empowered.
   • Costs: lack of standardisation, limited achievement of organisational goals, support/ guidance only given when requested.

PAGE 94

1. • Staff turnover (the number of people leaving the organisation) will decrease which will reduce costs associated with recruitment, selection, training and development.
   • The number of days staff are absent will reduce which means productivity will be higher and more customer needs can be satisfied.
   • Employees will be more motivated and happier at work which will result in customers receiving a better standard of service that will encourage them to return and also to provide positive feedback about the organisation.
   • Employees will be more willing to accept and adapt to any changes in the organisation as a result of the changing business environment; this will make implementing decisions easier as staff are not resistant to them.

2. • Staff turnover will increase which will cost the organisation money to find replacements.
   • Absence rates will increase resulting in lower productivity.
   • Employees will be less motivated resulting in poor customer service.
   • Change in the organisation might be harder to implement meaning decisions take longer to implement.

3. Trade unions represent the views of employees on different employment-related matters.

4. A works council is formed with representatives from across the organisation. It has the ability to access various types of information that relate to the organisation and it has the authority to take part alongside management in making decisions that relate to the workforce.

5. • There has been an increase in employment opportunities in the tertiary and quaternary sector at the same time as a decrease in the primary and secondary sector.
   • More people are becoming employed on part-time and temporary contracts compared to full-time or permanent ones to meet the needs of organisations that have to operate in a changing business and economic environment.
   • More women are now in employment in both full-time and part-time jobs and there has also been an increase in the number of women who have management positions.
   • Developments in technology have allowed more people to work out of the office, either as homeworkers or teleworkers.
   • The Government has encouraged people to become enterprising and as a result people are opting to become self-employed.
   • There has been an increase in the number of small businesses opening up because of the increase in people starting their own business.

6. **Advantages**

   • The organisation can recruit a wider range of employees.
   • Employees will be more motivated and therefore productivity will be higher.

   Disadvantages

   • Could be costly to implement lots of different types of flexible working practices.
   • May not always be possible to meet everyone's needs at the same time as the organisation's.

7. • Hot-desking – sharing a desk with others, booked when needed.
   • Teleworking – working outwith the organisation using technology to communicate.
   • Job-share – a full-time job is shared between two people.
   • Annualised hours – working a certain number of hours over the whole year, rather than a specific amount per day or week.
   • Flexi time – the employee has flexibility in their start and finish time but must usually work specific 'core hours'.

8.

Strike	Employees refuse to enter the workplace. They might have a picket line or demonstration outside the business to raise awareness of the issues they are facing.
Work to Rule	Employees only carry out the tasks and duties written in their job description and no other tasks are performed.
Sit In	Employees refuse to work and 'sit in' the workplace.
Go Slow	Employees work slower than normal in order to reduce productivity.
Overtime Ban	No hours above the minimum required (as per the employee's contract) are worked.
Boycott	Employees refuse to carry out a new task or to use a new piece of machinery.
Demonstration	A gathering of people raising awareness of a particular issue.

9. A job no longer exists.

10. An employee complaint regarding a work-related issue.

11. • Complaint needs to be investigated by following the organisation's grievance procedure.
  • May have to consult ACAS.
  • Motivation might be lower until issue is resolved.

12. An independent organisation that specialises in resolving disputes and disagreements between employees and their employer.

13.

Advantages	Disadvantages
• Employees who have the potential for promotion can be identified which can be motivating for them • Feedback is given to the employee by their line manager to improve their work; praise can be given for work done well – this is motivating • Can be a motivating experience if the appraisal is positive which increases productivity • Opportunities for CPD and training can be identified meaning people can do their jobs better • Targets for future performance can be discussed and agreed so that the employee has something to work towards	• Some employees might see the appraisal as a 'tick-box' exercise and not take it seriously or commit to it therefore wasting time • Can be a demotivating experience if the appraisal is negative therefore productivity decreases • It is a time consuming process to carry out; other activities are not being completed when an appraisal meeting is taking place and it is therefore costly and productivity decreases • An employee might have too many development needs which could result in additional stress for them and an increased workload

14. • **Peer-to-peer appraisal** – when a colleague at the same level of the hierarchy conducts the appraisal.
  • **360 degree appraisal** – when the skills and performance of an employee are compared against others who work around them using a thorough self-evaluation process.
  • **Informal appraisal** – no formal structure is followed; instead a chat between employee and employer is had.

PAGE 101

1. The role of the finance department in an organisation is to:

Control costs and expenses

Costs and expenses must be controlled to avoid financial problems and the need to borrow money to cover these costs. Where necessary, management might have to take action to reduce costs and the amount of money going out of the organisation.

Monitor cash flow going in and out of the business

Money coming into the organisation and going out of the organisation needs to be monitored. There needs to be enough 'cash' available to be able to pay suppliers, creditors and employees' wages. Making profit and having a good cash flow are two different things.

Forecast what might happen in the future

Preparing budgets and looking at past financial records can help to identify trends and to see what might happen in the future. Action can be taken if necessary to avoid financial problems.

Monitor performance

Financial information can be used to compare one year against a previous year to see if performance has improved. This is useful to see if action taken in the past has worked and, where necessary, to take action in the future. Ratio analysis can be used to help monitor performance.

Provide information for decision-making

We already know that managers make lots of decisions. Financial information plays a crucial role in their decision-making and will often influence which course of action is taken.

2. See the table on page 99.

3. • How motivated staff are.
   • The impact of external factors.
   • How successful has been in increasing market share the business.
   • The stage of the product life cycle.

4. **Issue additional shares**

   Limited companies could issue extra shares to new or existing shareholders. Plcs can sell their shares on the stock market.

   Leasing

   Leasing means to rent. Businesses could rent equipment or premises rather than buying these outright.

   Venture Capitalists (or Business Angels)

   Venture capitalists provide large loans to organisations that a bank or other lender may feel are too risky. They usually part-own the organisation in return for taking the risk.

5. See the tables on page 100-101.

PAGE 105

1. To forecast the amount of money expected to be received or paid out over a period of time.

2. • To show if the business will have a surplus (more cash expected to come in than go out) or deficit (more cash expected to go out than come in) so that action can be taken to manage cash flow.
   • It can show if additional finance is required to ensure the business continues to operate effectively.
   • It can help control expenses by highlighting periods when expenses could be high therefore making sure the business has necessary money available to cover these.
   • Can help in making decisions, for example, whether to launch into a new product, so that the organisation makes the best decisions it can.

3. • Bills cannot be paid.
   • A poor image might be given to suppliers and other creditors.
   • Decisions cannot be made.
   • Objectives might not be achieved.

4. See the table on page 102 for methods and justifications.

PAGE 111

1. This shows a summary of the money that has came in and gone out of the organisation over the past financial year. The **Trading Account** shows the **Gross Profit** whereas the **Profit and Loss Account** shows the **Net Profit.**

2. The Balance Sheet shows the value (worth) of an organisation at a particular point in time. It shows what the organisation owns (assets) and what debts (liabilities) it has.

3. Gross profit – profit after buying and selling.

   Net profit – profit after other income has been added to gross profit and expenses deducted.

   Debtors – people who owe the organisation money.

   Creditors – people whom the organisation owes money.

   Working capital – how easily an organisation can pay its short-term debts.

   Dividends – payments to shareholders for having shares in a company.

4. Bank, closing stock, debtors, cash

5. Creditors, bank overdraft

6. Wages, rent, electricity, advertising, insurance, rates

7. Through selling shares on the stock market.

8. • Spreadsheets could be used to store details of expenses and to create different financial statements.
   • Spreadsheets could be used to create graphs to show sales figures in different branches/ stores.
   • Specialist packages, for example, eg SAGE accounting, could be used to record financial transactions.

Unit 3 : Management of Marketing and Operations

PAGE 129

1.

Segment	What it is
Gender	Segmenting by gender means to market a product towards a specific gender ie male or female.
Age	Segmenting by age means to market a product towards people of a certain age group eg holidays for 18-30 year olds
Occupation	Segmenting by occupation means to market a product towards people who do a particular job eg stethoscope for doctors
Religious or cultural belief	Segmenting by religious or cultural belief means to market a product towards people who follow a specific religious or cultural faith.
Income/Social class	Segmenting by income or social class means to market a product towards people who have a certain level of income or belong to a particular social group (eg working or upper class).
Geographical location	Segmenting by geographical location means to market a product towards people who live in a particular location eg sun cream for hot locations!
Lifestyle	Segmenting by lifestyle means to market a product towards people who lead a particular life eg if they are into sport and fitness.

2.

Market-led (market orientated)	Product-led (product orientated)
• Product produced based on what the customer wants • Customer wants and needs are identified through market research • Changes in social factors (eg trends and fashion) can be identified and acted upon more easily • The market may have significant competition	• Product produced because the organisation thinks it is good at providing it • Little or no market research carried out as the needs and wants of the customer are not of importance • The market may have little or no competition

3. Differentiated marketing – marketing products towards a particular market segment
Undifferentiated marketing – focusing on more than one target market

4. • To develop a successful marketing strategy.
   • To make decisions about the product the organisation offers.

5. • Why do they buy what they do?
   • What motivates them to buy?
   • What influences buying decisions?
   • What type of customer buys the product?
   • Where do they choose to buy? Why?
   • What do they look for when buying?

6.

Impulse purchases	Buying something without thinking, often in the spur of the moment. It might be because something has influenced the customer to buy (eg a promotion).
Routine purchases	Buying something because it is habit eg going to buy a loaf of bread. These types of purchases will happen without much thought.
Limited decision-making purchases	Buying something that requires some thought before a decision is made. For example, thinking about whether or not a piece of clothing is appropriate for a certain purpose.
Extensive decision-making purchases	Buying something that requires a high degree of thought before a decision is made. For example, buying a new car or a house. These types of purchases might not be made very often.

7. Electronic point of sale systems (EPOS) can gather information about consumer behaviour that the organisation can attempt to analyse and understand.

- When people make purchases in a supermarket or shop, the EPOS system is collecting data about them and their buying habits.
- Promotions, offers and mailshots can then be designed specifically for them.

PAGE 134

1. Attempting to find out what customers want and what is happening in the marketplace.

It involves looking at existing information and gathering new information.

2. Field research involves gathering new information whereas desk research involves looking at existing information.

3. Websites, newspapers/magazines, government reports, textbooks

4. Surveys, interviews, observations, hall tests, focus groups

5.
- Products can be adapted to meet customer requirements.
- Products can be tested by customers to gain their reactions.
- Information can be used to ensure the correct market segment is being targeted.
- It evaluates how effective a marketing campaign is.

6. Questionnaires – asking people's views and opinions to see whether or not they like something. This is a good way of asking a lot of people for their views, particularly if done online or through the post, and is inexpensive compared to, for example, eg observations.

Observations – watching people and recording their behaviour towards something. This information can be analysed quickly as it is often quantitative. People usually react naturally as they are often unaware they are being observed.

Hall tests – allowing customers to try out a product. First hand information is gathered.

Focus groups – a discussion between a selected number of people and a researcher. People's feelings towards different topics can be gathered as a discussion is taking place.

7. Primary information is new information gathered for a specific purpose whereas secondary information is old information gathered for another purpose.

8. Internal information is information from within the organisation, eg sales figures, whereas external information is from outwith the organisation, eg Government reports or competitors, websites.

9. • Random sampling – randomly selecting people from a list, eg a telephone book. These individuals must then be questioned.

   • Quota sampling – selecting people to question based on certain characteristics, eg age, gender or occupation.

10. • Surveys could be created and distributed via a website.

    • Spreadsheets could be used to analyse research data.

PAGE 137

1. Because organisations are now so closely focused on their customers.

2. • **Process** – the different processes and systems used to deliver the service being provided.
   • **People** – those involved in providing the service to customers, eg staff.
   • **Physical Evidence** – the location of where the service is being offered and what it looks like, eg store layout and design

3. • Process – for example, the 'drive-thru' eg McDonalds example given on page 136.
   • People – staff serving customers.
   • Physical evidence – store layout and design.

4. • Price – promotional pricing could be used to encourage customers.
   • Product – the product could be adapted or changed (eg new features added) to make it more appealing to customers.
   • Place – the product could be sold in more locations to make it more accessible.
   • Promotion – advertising methods could be changed or increased to target a wider range of people.

PAGE 141

1. The actual good or service being sold.

2.

Development	Research and development of the product. A number of activities are carried out (eg market research, test marketing, prototype is built).
Introduction	Product is launched onto the market. Product is heavily advertised and sales will begin to increase.
Growth	The product has gained greater awareness and sales grow rapidly.
Maturity	Sales are at a peak and the product is well known in the marketplace. Extension strategies might be used at this stage to keep sales at a peak.

(continued)

Saturation	The end of maturity; everyone has the product and is no longer demanding it. This might be a single point of time or it might be for longer.
Decline	Sales decline as newer and better products are introduced to the market. The product is no longer wanted. Product is eventually withdrawn.

3.

Development	No sales, high costs. No profit.
Introduction	Sales are low and costs are high. Very little or no profit.
Growth	Sales grow rapidly and profit begins to increase.
Maturity	High profits.
Saturation	High profits before they decrease.
Decline	Profits fall and a loss might be incurred eventually.

4. Methods used to try and stimulate sales and encourage people to buy.

5. • Changing the appearance of the packaging to give the product a new image.
   • Changing the size, variety or shape of the product as this makes it different from the original.
   • Improving the quality of the finished product by, for example, using higher quality raw materials.
   • Changing the method of promotion used to promote the product, for example, by offering a discount.
   • Changing the method of advertising the product to reach a larger number of people.
   • Changing the price of the product (up or down), to reach a different market segment.
   • Changing the place the product is sold eg offering it online as well as in a shop.
   • Changing the name of the product.
   • Changing the use of the product so that it can be used for different purposes.

6. Range of products being offered.

7. **Benefits**

   • To reduce risk of failure of one product as one product might be doing better than another.
   • To appeal to a variety of market segments as different products will appeal to different types of customers.
   • To increase sales and profits from selling different products as customers will be able to buy a variety of products from the same business.
   • To make introducing a new product easier since customers will already be aware of the business.
   • To cope with products that are only demanded in certain seasons as other products will gain sales at different times of the year.

   Costs

   • Costs of promoting and advertising lots of different products could be high and could result in less profit.
   • If one product receives a bad reputation or image this might impact upon all the products being sold by the business.
   • Maintaining a varied product portfolio will involve a high cost of research and development.

- Cost of purchasing and maintaining machinery for different types of products might be high.
- Staff may require training on the features of different products which could be time consuming and expensive.

8. • Used to plot the range of products offered by an organisation.

   - Shows the position of a product in relation to its market share and whether it is achieving market growth.
   - Four components: problem child/question marks, star, dog, cash flow
   - See diagram on page 140.

PAGE 143

1. The amount charged to the customer to purchase the good or service.

2. Low price is when the price charged is lower than competitors and high price is when the price charged is higher than competitors.

3. Destroyer – this forces competitors out of the market so that the business can then charge higher prices at a later date.

   Skimming – a high price can be charged because little or no competition exists. A large profit can be made.

   Psychological – this method tricks people into thinking the product is cheaper than it is and attracts them to buy it. Attracts consumers who buy on impulse.

   Competitive – attracts customers and allows businesses to compete.

   Cost-plus – ensures that the cost of making the product is covered and that a profit is also made.

4. Skimming – a high price can be charged because little or no competition exists.

5. Premium pricing – the high price gives the product a unique and exclusive image.

6. • The life cycle of the product.
   - The price charged by competitors.
   - How much it costs to make the product.
   - How much profit is wanted.
   - How much of the product can be supplied.
   - The market segment that the product is focused towards.

7. To remain competitive.

PAGE 148

1. Channel of distribution is the route a product will follow to get from the manufacturer to the customer.

2. • The actual product and its life cycle.
   - The image and exclusivity the manufacturer wants the product to have.
   - The availability of finance.

- The reputation and reliability of wholesalers and retailers.
- Legal restrictions.
- The logistic facilities available by the manufacturer (how able it is to transport and store the product from one place to the next).

3.
- A wholesaler buys large quantities of items from the manufacturer and then sells them on to retailers, or directly to the customer, in smaller quantities.
- A retailer is an organisation that distributes products to the customer on behalf of the manufacturer.

4.

Advantages	Disadvantages
• Distribution and storage costs are reduced because products might be bought in bulk • The wholesaler may promote the manufactured product resulting in less cost for the manufacturer • Risk of not selling the product to a retailer or to the customer is taken on by the wholesaler and therefore risk for the manufacturer is reduced • Packaging, labelling and marketing might be carried out by the wholesaler • The manufacturer does not have to worry about having to sell excess stock if there are changes in the business environment (eg fashion) • The wholesaler may provide information on the product for the retailer • Retailers do not have to pay for expensive storage facilities to hold stock as they can buy smaller quantities compared to sourcing directly from the manufacturer	• The manufacturer loses control over what happens to the product after they have sold it and may not like the way the product is being portrayed by wholesalers or retailers • There is less profit for the manufacturer as they have not sold directly to the customer • Loyalty and any associated benefits of this (eg discounts) with the manufacturer cannot be gained

5. **Advantages**

- Retailer decides on price.
- Retailer decides how to display product.
- Retailers stock a range of products.
- Retailers can offer extra services, eg credit facilities and deliveries.
- Retailers can take advantage of buying in bulk.

Disadvantages

- Product might face competition from other manufacturers.
- Extra financial costs associated with using a retailer.

6.

Supermarkets	Often very large organisations that buy large quantities and then sell them in their stores.
Discount Retailer	They tend to provide non-branded products at a cheap price.
E-tailer	Shopping online and having the product delivered to you (eg through Amazon).
Convenience Retailer	Often referred to as the corner shop. This type of retailer normally has a small shop where a limited number of products can be bought.

7. Examples will vary.

8. A system of warehouses and transport to get the product from the manufacturer to the customer.

9. See pages 147-148.

10. See pages 147-148.

PAGE 151

1. Above the line – mass media promotions.

   Below the line – promotions to focused groups of people.

2. Into the pipeline – promotions to encourage retailers to stock products.

   Out of the pipeline – promotions to encourage customers to buy from a retailer.

3. Above the line – newspaper advertising, radio advertising, billboards, internet websites, celebrity endorsement (NB make sure you describe each one).

   Below the line – special offers/sales promotions, PR activities.

4. Depends on answer chosen in Q3. May require revision from National 5.

5. Into the pipeline – point of sale materials, sale or return, staff training, dealer loaders.

   Out of the pipeline – free samples, loyalty schemes, vouchers, special offers.

6. Depends on answer chosen in Q5.

7. Attempts to improve the relationship and communication between the public and an organisation.

8.

Press releases	A press release is usually a written statement to the press (eg newspapers and TV stations) that communicates activities within the organisation.
Sponsorships	Organisations may sponsor events where there is likely to be a lot of public attention. Sport and charity events are often sponsored by large organisations which have their company name displayed on material that the sport or charity is distributing. Football strips sponsored by companies are a good example.
Charity donations	Organisations may donate sums of money to charities in the hope of not only helping a good cause, but also being seen as socially responsible. This will raise awareness of the organisation.

9. • Websites for internet advertising.
   • Social media for interacting with customers.
   • E-mail for mailshots.
   • Use of special offer websites to promote products (eg Groupon).

PAGE 157

1. • Quality of raw materials
    • Lead time
    • Quantity of raw materials
    • Location of supplier
    • Reliability and reputation of supplier
    • Storage space available

2. • Ensure stock is readily available at any one time.
    • Ensure production continues.
    • Avoid delays to customer orders.
    • Ensure over-stocking does not take place, which results in higher costs.
    • Avoid stock deteriorating (eg fresh food) and/or becoming obsolete.

3. • Increased financial costs (eg storage, security and insurance).
    • Stock could go to waste or deteriorate resulting in stock that needs to be discarded.
    • Higher risk of stock being stolen.

4. • Production could stop and therefore employees and machines could be sitting idle.
    • Customers might not receive their orders on time which could result in complaints.
    • The business could gain a poor reputation and image.

5. • **Maximum stock level** – the highest amount of stock that can be stored at one time. At this level stock costs will be at the minimum per unit because the organisation is at full capacity.
    • **Minimum stock level** – the lowest amount of stock that should be stored at one time. At this level there is a danger that stock levels could be too low and production could stop.
    • **Re-order level** – the quantity at which more stock is ordered.
    • **Re-order quantity** – the quantity of stock that has to be ordered to bring levels back to the maximum stock level.
    • **Lead time** – the time that passes between ordering stock and it arriving.
    See diagram on page 154

6. • **Centralised storage** – storing stock in one place.
    • **Decentralised storage** – storing stock in more than one place.

7. Just in time (JIT) is a method of stock control that keeps cost levels to the minimum. As the name suggests, stock arrives *just in time* for it to be used in the production process and goods are only manufactured when a customer order is received.

8. **Advantages**

    • Less cash is tied up in stock.
    • Less storage and warehouse space is required.
    • Wastage should be reduced as only stock required is ordered.
    • Changes in the external environment (eg fashion trends) will have a reduced impact.

    Disadvantages

    • Suppliers who are reliable are required so that stock is delivered on time.
    • Production can stop if stock is not delivered when required.

- Less environmentally friendly as more journeys with less stock will be made.
- Delivery costs might be higher due to more journeys.
- Discounts for bulk buying (economies of scale) might be lost.

9. A warehouse is the name given to the place where finished products are held until they are ready to be distributed to the customer.

10. A system of warehouses and transport to get the product from the manufacturer to the customer.

11. • Reliability of other organisations
   - Legal restrictions
   - Availability of finance
   - The product being distributed
   - The image associated with the product
   - The stock management system being used
   - The distribution capability of the manufacturer

PAGE 161

1. **Job production** is when one product is made from start to finish before another one is made. The product is made to the customer's own requirements and this results in a unique or one-off product being made. Products made by job production are usually made by hand by someone who is very skilled at what they are doing.

   Batch production is when one group of identical products is made at any one time. All products in the batch move onto the next stage of production at the same time. Machinery and equipment can be cleaned and/or changed between batches to produce a different product. Batch production is often used when manufacturing a product that comes in different varieties, styles or sizes.

   Flow production (sometimes known as line production) is when parts are added to the product as it moves along the production line. The final product will have been made by the time it reaches the end of the production line. Flow production is sometimes called line production.

2. • Job production – wedding cakes, handmade chocolates, pieces of art, sandwiches made to order in a sandwich shop.
   - Batch production – cakes, newspapers/magazines, bread.
   - Flow production – cars/vans, computers and other electrical items.

3. See pages 158-159.

4. Labour intensive – use of employees in production.

   Capital intensive – use of machinery in production.

5.

Advantages	Disadvantages
• Employees can use their initiative when required • There is always a supply of labour available (though highly skilled employees might be more difficult to source) • Cheaper than purchasing and maintaining equipment	• It costs money to recruit, select and train new employees • The accuracy and the quality of work from person to person can vary

6.

Advantages	Disadvantages
• Machines can work 24/7 without the need for breaks • Machines can produce a consistent and standardised accuracy and quality of work	• Individual customer requirements cannot be met • Breakdowns can occur which can be expensive • Employees become tired and bored of repetitive tasks that might need to be carried out

7. Mechanisation means that there is some capital as well as some labour involved in production, eg people working machines.

8. Automation means that capital has replaced the need for humans to carry out the work required because machines, equipment and technology can do it instead.

PAGE 169

1. • Quality control – checking the product's quality once it has been made.
   • Quality assurance – checking the product's quality during production.
   • Quality management – a total commitment towards quality from the organisation and its employees. Aims for perfection every time.
   • Benchmarking – comparing a product against the best in the market and trying to match this standard.
   • Mystery shopping – a person who makes a visit to a shop, buys something and then feeds back to the organisation. Employees won't know who the mystery shopper is.
   • Quality symbol – an award given to an organisation when it meets a particular specification or set of criteria. The symbol will usually appear on the product.

2. • Quality control – cheaper than other methods.
   • Quality assurance – faults can be discovered before the product reaches the end of the production process.
   • Quality management – a total commitment towards quality from everyone in the organisation, aiming to be the best.
   • Benchmarking – allows the organisation to be competitive.
   • Mystery shopping – unknown shopper so they will experience the shop and its customer service first hand. Accurate representation.
   • Quality symbol – recognised symbol awarded.

3. • Suppliers have produced or obtained their raw materials in an ethical manner.
   • The fair trade symbol that is on fair trade products means that those who have produced the product (eg farmers) have received a fair price for their product.

- The supplier will treat their employees fairly and will have a commitment towards their welfare and health & safety.
- The fair trade symbol is owned by Fairtrade International and is an independent assurance that the organisation is adopting a fair trade approach to business.

4. Recycling, being sustainable, minimise packaging, preventing pollution, using renewable energy sources, energy saving strategies

5. See pages 164–166.

6.
- CAD – computer-aided design – used in the research and design stage of a new product before it is manufactured.
- CAM – computer-aided manufacture – involves using computer-controlled equipment and robots in the manufacturing of a product (ie automation).

7.
- Computer facilities (eg computer and internet) could be used for purchasing materials online.
- E-mail can be used to confirm an order has been received and to let the customer know about the progress and status of the order (eg when it has been dispatched).
- Websites could be used to compare the prices of different suppliers before deciding which one to purchase.
- Deliveries could be tracked and traced via logistical companies' websites.
- Computer programs (eg a database or spreadsheet) could be used to store stock levels.
- EPOS can provide automatic updates on stock and sales levels.
- Computer-aided design (CAD) can be used in the research and design stage of a new product before it is manufactured.
- Computer-aided manufacture (CAM) involves using computer-controlled equipment and robots in the manufacturing of a product (ie automation).

© 2014 Leckie & Leckie Ltd
Cover © ink-tank and associates

001/14052014

10 9 8 7 6 5 4 3

ISBN 9780007549351

Published by
Leckie & Leckie Ltd
An imprint of HarperCollins*Publishers*
Westerhill Road, Bishopbriggs, Glasgow, G64 2QT
T: 0844 576 8126   F: 0844 576 8131
leckieandleckie@harpercollins.co.uk   www.leckieandleckie.co.uk

Special thanks to
Rona Gloag (proofread)
Jennifer Richards (proofread)
Jouve (layout and illustrations)

Dedicated to Rob Jackson

A CIP Catalogue record for this book is available from the British Library.

Acknowledgements

We would like to thank the following for permission to reproduce their material:
P5 © Getty Images, P23 © Martin Good/Shutterstock.com, P33 © Chris Parypa Photography/Shutterstock.com, © i4lcocl2/Shutterstock.com, P129 © joyfull/Shutterstock.com, P146 Tesco - This file is licensed under the Creative Commons Attribution 3.0 Unported license, P146 Poundland - This work is licensed under the Creative Commons Attribution-ShareAlike 3.0 License, P146 corner shop - This file is licensed under the Creative Commons Attribution 2.0 Generic license, P167 © Tupungato/Shutterstock.com

All other images from Shutterstock.

Whilst every effort has been made to trace the copyright holders, in cases where this has been unsuccessful, or if any have inadvertently been overlooked, the Publishers would gladly receive any information enabling them to rectify any error or omission at the first opportunity.